MARCO ⊕ POLO
THAILAND

with Local Tips

*The author's special recommendations are
highlighted in yellow throughout this guide*

GW00707905

There are five symbols to help you find your way around this guide:

Marco Polo's top recommendations – the best in each category

sites with a scenic view

places where the local people meet

places where young people get together

(98/A1)
pages and coordinates for the Road Atlas of Thailand
(U/A1) *coordinates for the City Map of Bangkok inside back cover*
(O) *area not covered by the City Map of Bangkok*

*This guide was written by journalist Wilfried Hahn. Since 1987 he has
spent several months each year in Thailand and is the South-east Asia
correspondent for a German travel magazine.*

MARCO ⊕ POLO

Travel guides and language guides in this series:

Alaska • Algarve • Amsterdam • Australia/Sydney • Bahamas • Barbados
Barcelona • Berlin • Brittany • Brussels • California • Canada • Channel
Islands • Chicago and the Great Lakes • Costa Brava/Barcelona • Costa del
Sol/Granada • Côte d'Azur • Crete • Cuba • Cyprus • Dominican Republic
Eastern Canada • Eastern USA • Egypt • Florence • Florida • Gran Canaria • Greek
Islands/Aegean • Hong Kong • Ibiza/Formentera • Ireland • Israel • Istanbul
Lanzarote • London • Los Angeles • Madeira • Mallorca • Malta • Mexico • Minorca
New York • New Zealand • Normandy • Norway • Paris • Portugal • Prague
Rhodes • Rocky Mountains • Rome • San Francisco • Scotland • South Africa
Southwestern USA • Tenerife • Thailand • Turkish Coast • Tuscany
USA: New England • USA: Southern States • Venice • Washington D.C.
Western Canada • Western USA

French • German • Italian • Spanish

Marco Polo would be very interested to hear your
comments and suggestions. Please write to:

North America:
Marco Polo North America
70 Bloor Street East
Oshawa, Ontario, Canada
(B) 905-436-2525

United Kingdom:
GeoCenter International Ltd
The Viables Centre
Harrow Way
Basingstoke, Hants RG22 4BJ

Our authors have done their research very carefully, but should any errors or omissions
have occurred, the publisher cannot be held responsible for any injury, damage
or inconvenience suffered due to incorrect information in this guide

Cover photograph: Wat Phra Keo in Bangkok (Image Bank: Montgomery)
Photos: Author (36, 39, 41, 47, 49, 51, 64, 67); K. H. Buschmann (20, 24, 60); W. Hahn: Zürn (69);
Mauritius: Beck (28, 63), Cassio (54), Hubatka (97), Vidler (27); O. Stadler (4, 15, 77, 80, 93);
O. Stadler & A. Stubhan (18); H. Wormsbächer (6); M. Thomas (11, 12, 32, 44, 72)

1ˢᵗ edition 2000
© Mairs Geographischer Verlag, Ostfildern, Germany
Translator: Wendy Bell
English edition 2000: Peter Bell
Editorial director: Ferdinand Ranft
Chief editor: Marion Zorn
Cartography for the Road Atlas: © Mairs Geographischer Verlag
Design and layout: Thienhaus/Wippermann
Printed in Germany

All rights reserved. No part of this publication may be reproduced or transmitted in any form
or by any means, electronic or mechanical including photocopying, recording or by any information
storage and retrieval systems without prior permission from the publisher

CONTENTS

Discover Thailand!

Magnificent temples, mountain adventure tours and magical beaches: the kingdom of Thailand is a fascinating place to travel in – and a land of smiles

A farming village in the far north-east of Thailand. It lies in the midst of rice fields which stretch away to the horizon, like a forgotten island in the ocean. Pile dwellings huddle beneath the coconut palms. Inside the houses crockery clinks and clatters, while, underneath, the water buffalo doze. A monk wends his way along the dusty village street. Even in the twilight betwixt night and day, his orange-coloured robe seems to glisten and shine. An old woman, kneeling in front of her house, begs the monk to accept her gift. She cannot spare a lot. A small plastic bag of rice and two hard-boiled eggs. The monk remains standing, holding his alms bowl out to her. He utters no word of thanks. It is for the giver to say thank you, for she has received the opportunity to do good. But the young Buddhist monk blesses the woman, who remains kneeling with hands folded until his back is turned on her. Then she rises, shaking the dry dust from her sarong, and somewhere a cock crows to the rising sun. The woman climbs

Mobile snack stands like this are part of the street scene everywhere in Thailand

the steps to her house. Before stooping to pass under the low corrugated tin roof into the space which serves as living room, bedroom and kitchen all in one, she turns once again. She looks into the distance, towards where the rice fields conceal an asphalt road. The road goes to Korat, the provincial capital, and then on to Bangkok, the vast and sprawling Thai capital where her son is working as a taxi driver.

Perhaps at this very moment he is stuck in the morning rush-hour traffic, winding down his window as he waits to buy a garland of jasmine and rose petals from an itinerant flower seller – a fragrant talisman for the rear-view mirror of his over-worked cab. The day in Bangkok is heralded not only by the cock crow but by horrendous traffic jams. But the taxi driver takes it all in his stride, no road rage here. Patience after all is a Buddhist virtue. Life is much too short to get over-excited about petty things. He sticks a little bronze Buddha onto the dashboard. Soon no doubt he will know just why the Buddha is smiling.

It makes not a jot of difference whether you are imbibing the tranquility of a Thai village or caught up in a Bangkok traffic jam: you will soon discover that this is a country like no other. A land of contrasts, full of mystery, an exotic land. And yet you won't feel a stranger for long, for this is also a land of smiles. The ease and serenity with which Thais accept their lot, the way in which they confront adversity in everyday life with a smile, can convey a longer lasting impression than any shining golden temple or palm-shaded beach. More than anything else it is its people which have turned Thailand into Asia's number one holiday destination.

In the course of its history Thailand has already absorbed many newcomers, from Chinese to Indians and from Laotians to hill tribes. Even the Thais themselves only arrived here as migrants from the south of China between the 8th and the 11th century. And before they were able to establish their first kingdom in Sukhothai in 1238, they

Many young men spend a few weeks to several months as monks in a monastery

had first to end the supremacy of the Khmer, the dominant people here in the 11th and 12th centuries. But the new masters did not consider themselves a master race. They did not immediately set out to destroy the cultures of the Khmer and the Mon, whose Dvaravati kingdom extended over central Thailand from the 6th to the 11th century. Instead they absorbed this legacy and built their own upon it. So in the veins of the Thais flows the blood of those Asiatic tribes who were there before them, and of those who came after them too. The only people with whom they did not mix – until, that is, the era of long-distance travel – were the *falang*, the white-skinned foreigners from Europe. It is true that as early as 1512 Portuguese traders paddled up the Chao Phraya River to Ayutthaya, the second most important city in the kingdom of Siam after Sukhothai further to the north; and a Greek by the name of Constantine Phaulkon even acquired an important position at court. But in 1688 when the intrigues of the delegations of Dutchmen, Britons and Frenchmen, each competing with the others for influence, became too burdensome for the Siamese, they beheaded the Greek power-broker, sent the other Europeans packing, and sealed off their country from the West. King Mongkut, whose reign lasted from 1851 to 1868, was the first Thai monarch to encourage the re-establishment of links with Europe and America.

His son and successor Chulalongkorn (r. 1868–1910) was a great modernizer like his father.

He sent young Thais to be educated in Europe, had a railway built opening up the north of the country, and abolished slavery. He also decreed that his subjects must adopt family names.

Despite the fact that the Thais are always anxious for reconciliation and prefer to come to an accommodation rather than reach for arms, there was a time when they nevertheless suffered badly at the hands of one of their Asiatic neighbours. In 1767 – a date which every school child learns and etched in the memory of every Thai – the Burmese reduced Ayutthaya, one of the most brilliant Asian cities of the period, to rubble and ashes. Quite possibly this national catastrophe was the principal reason why, in the century that followed, Siam did everything in its power to remain independent and intact. When the nations of Europe returned once again to the Far East with the express intention of dividing this part of the world among themselves too, Siam was the only country in South-East Asia to avoid falling under the colonial yoke. By exploiting the fact that it was very much in the interests of the British in Burma (present day Myanmar) and Malaya (Malaysia), and of the French in Cambodia and Laos, to have a buffer state separating their respective spheres of influence, the Siamese kingdom survived largely untouched, ceding just one or two border areas.

Flexible as the bamboo which bends in the wind in order not to break, the nation which in 1939 gave Thailand (Land of the Free) its name, also manoeuvred its way diplomatically through the turbulent period of the Second World War. Instead of quarreling with the immensely powerful Japanese, the Thais preferred to enter officially into an alliance with them. As a result, not a shot was fired when the troops of Tenno, the Japanese Emperor, entered their country with a workforce consisting of allied prisoners of war and Asian forced labour to construct a supply route to Burma over the now infamous bridge across the Kwai. But at the same time, the then ambassador in Washington and later prime minister, Seni Pramoj, simply left his country's formal declaration of war against the USA lying undelivered in his desk drawer.

Thailand's post war history has been dominated by a succession of generals who wrestled for political control and organized repeated coups. Student protests in 1973 and 1976 were violently suppressed. But the economic boom of the nineteen eighties not only transformed the Bangkok skyline but the country's political landscape as well. In the capital in particular a more broadly-based middle class began to emerge, quickly developing a political consciousness and demanding a say in the shaping of affairs. In 1992, when General Suchinda allowed himself to be elected premier by the compliant deputies, it was not just students who took to the streets. They were joined by bank employees, craftsmen, housewives and merchants. Shots were fired around the Democratic Memorial and barricades set alight. Finally the King, who normally distances himself from day-to-day politics,

History at a glance

From 3500 BC
Ban Chiang in north-east Thailand is settled by a farming people who have already mastered pottery and working in bronze

8th–11th century
The Thais migrate from southern China

11th–12th century
Virtually the whole of Thailand is under Cambodian Khmer rule

1238
The Thais succeed in breaking the power of the Khmer. Sukhothai becomes the capital of the first Thai kingdom

1275–1317
King Ramkhamhaeng, "Father of the Thais", turns Sukhothai into a powerful kingdom. He develops the Thai alphabet, also promoting foreign trade, the arts and the spread of Buddhism

1350
A new kingdom is created in Ayutthaya; Sukhothai loses its former dominance

1512
Portuguese merchants arrive in Ayutthaya, the first of the Europeans. They are soon followed by the Dutch, British and French

1767
The Burmese capture Ayutthaya. The magnificent capital is completely destroyed

1782
King Chakri, Rama I, founds the Chakri dynasty, making the village of Bangkok his new capital

1868–1910
King Chulalongkorn, Rama V, sends Thais to be educated in Europe and abolishes slavery

1932
Bloodless coup d'état. The absolute monarchy is abolished and replaced by a constitutional one

1939
Siam adopts a new name, "Thailand" (Land of the Free)

1946
The present monarch, King Bhumibol Adulyadej, ascends the throne as Rama IX. In 1988 his reign becomes the longest in Thai history

1973
The military government violently suppresses student protest and is forced to resign

1980–1988
General Prem Tinsulanonda is Prime Minister at the head of a coalition government. Thailand experiences an economic boom

1992
Mass protests take place after General Suchinda Kraprayoon seizes power

1997
Economic crisis in Asia brings the boom years to an abrupt end

1999
The International Monetary Fund endorses the programme of financial reform instituted by the coalition government, led once again by Chuan Leekpai. The economy stabilizes

took it upon himself to mediate. The whole nation sat in front of their television sets and witnessed the denouement. Rama IX, who though not an absolute monarch enjoys almost absolute authority, built up over a reign of more than 50 years, talked persuasively with both the general and the leader of the protest movement, Chamlong Srimuang, an ascetic and ex-governor of Bangkok. The soldiers returned to their barracks, Suchinda resigned, and the demonstrators resumed their studies or their work.

Giving ground and not taking confrontation to the very limit is a characteristic of the Thais, manifesting itself not only in the intrigues of those in positions of power but also in the contretemps of everyday life. Wherever possible Thais will always attempt to diffuse tension with a smile. They eschew interfering in other people's affairs, and expect others to do likewise. Open criticism is scorned, since it means the destruction of harmony and loss of face – the latter the worst thing that can befall any Thai.

With their positive attitude to life the Thais are not given to brooding over things. They have a saying *Kid mak, puat hua* – too much pondering only gives you a headache.

It is true that this people is not always easy to understand, certainly not by anyone whose head is full of Western ways of thinking. How, for example, is one to reconcile the fact that a nation who enthusiastically embrace everything and anything *tansamai* (modern), are also as superstitious as can be? Internet cafés are everywhere; but these same people, who with the click of a mouse eagerly surf the web, are apparently mortally afraid of spirits, to the extent that they build little houses on every street corner to placate them. Or even whole shrines.

The junction of Ploenchit, Rama I, Rajadamri and Rajaprarop Roads in Bangkok is jam-packed with cars, buses and lorries. Only the most expert of motor-cyclists, able to judge a gap to the millimetre, can find a way through. The whistles of the frantically gesticulating traffic policemen sound more like shrill cries for help. But even in the midst of this nightmare of modern times, exotic Thailand makes itself felt. No, that aroma of incense sticks and the strains of classical Thai music blending with the noise of engines are no hallucination. Nor are the delicate girl dancers resplendent in their glittering costumes. There they are, on the corner of Ploenchit and Rajadamri, dancing around a gilded statue, the base of which is hidden beneath a mass of votive garlands. With lotus blossom in their folded hands, schoolgirls kneel next to secretaries, and building workers next to bankers. They pray to be lucky in love, in their careers, at gambling. In the middle of the traffic stands the Erawan Shrine, with its gilded statue of the four-headed Hindu god, Brahma. Those entreating him for favours are actually practising Buddhists. But they don't for a moment consider themselves disloyal to their faith. Who says that a strange god only helps his own? Particularly since this one has already performed miracles. In 1956 when the Erawan Hotel was under construction (now rebuilt as the Grand Hyatt Erawan), several building workers were killed. The culprits were soon identified: the developers. They had driven the resident spirits from their hereditary patch, without any offer of a suitable alternative. To make amends and put things right, a shrine was erected next to the hotel. So the spirits need no longer wander about homeless, causing mischief.

The country is as varied as its society is complex. With an area of just 514,000 sq km, Thailand is roughly the same size as France. Geographically it is divided into four regions. The central plain with its fertile alluvial basin is the rice bowl of the country, while Bangkok and its one million inhabitants make it the main industrial centre too. Foothills of the Himalayas make up the mountainous north. Up there, where hill tribes in colourful costumes still practise slash and burn agriculture, the temperatures even in the winter months are high enough to permit the cultivation of strawberries and apples. Despite the barren soil, almost the whole of the drought-plagued plateau of the north-east is farmed. Of a total population of 61 million, as many as 20 million live here in the Isan, the country's poorhouse. In the villages most of the streets are dirt roads and people collect their water from wells and cisterns. If there is a little piece of chicken on the plate next to the rice then it must be a special day. Few tourists travel to the north-east. Yet it is precisely there that they should go if they want to experience the most traditional part of the country, where life is still governed by the rhythm of the seasons and the sowing and harvesting of crops.

But who can blame foreign visitors who, coming from much colder climes, are drawn to that part of the country which most fulfills their idea of the tropics, that is, to Thailand's south, extending like an elephant's trunk down to the Malaysian frontier. Pineapples grow in the fields, espaliers of rubber plants in the plantations, and coconut palms throw feathery shade upon cream-coloured beaches. Fisherfolk tie gaily coloured rags of cloth and garlands of blossom to the bows of their craft, and bougainvillea bushes set the gardens ablaze. In particular it is the islands of the south which, magically relaxing and a feast for all the senses, attract holidaymakers from all over the world.

The only city in Thailand to truly warrant the sobriquet "cosmopolitan" is the capital Bangkok. About one in seven Thais live here. At first sight this South-East Asian metropolis, with its highrise buildings and solid streams of cars, appears much like any other modern city. But as you take a closer look, you will soon find that here architectural styles are all thrown together higgledy-piggledy like the contents of a toy-box: there are skyscrapers painted in every conceivable shade, shopping precincts embellished with columns like Greek temples, and company offices which look like nothing so much as robots cast in concrete or as if assembled from huge Lego bricks. As far as its architecture is concerned, Bangkok gaily mixes everything and anything and shrinks from nothing. *Suey mak*, say the Thais – beautiful. Because they are almost as afraid of monotony and boredom as they are of spirits. Despite this dislike of dullness, the provincial towns offer quite a different picture from the capital. There was a time when only temples and palaces were built for eternity and in consequence they alone were constructed of stone; so it is only here and there that traditional wooden houses have survived Thailand's scramble to catch up with modernity. As a result, with their rows of faceless brick and concrete buildings, most of the country's smaller towns are largely indistinguishable from one another. Only on the island of Phuket do you still see elderly villas and shophouses in the old Sino-Portuguese style, a style strongly reminiscent of the colonial architecture of Georgetown on the Malaysian island of Penang.

Up until the Second World War a green canopy still covered almost all of Thailand: 70 per cent of the country was then forested. Elephants trumpeted in the jungle, tigers and leopards lay in wait for deer and wild boar. But a rapidly expanding population needed more and more agricultural land. The forests were cut down, replaced by paddy fields, rubber plantations, market gardens and orchards. Vast swathes of jungle were cleared to feed the insatiable timber and paper industries. Today the forested areas have shrunk to little more than 20 per cent of the total area. There are probably only about 2,000 wild elephants living in the jungle, and the number of big cats, now seriously threatened with extinction, is estimated at only a few hundred. Their reserves are just a handful of Thailand's 99 National Parks and conservation areas, which anyway

Elephants, symbols of luck and royal power, are becoming rare in Thailand

amount to no more than half the country's remaining forested land. Many tourists are disappointed because, on trekking tours in the mountains and excursions in the National Parks, they are seldom if ever fortunate enough to catch an elephant, never mind a tiger, in front of their camera lens.

That said, you don't have to resort to the zoo to discover Thailand's varied fauna. In the Gulf of Siam and in the Andaman Sea there are diving grounds which are among the best in South-East Asia. True, you have to be lucky to find yourself keeping pace with a huge, plankton-eating whale shark. But every diving school knows of places where you will be able almost to reach out and stroke the (equally harmless) spotted leopard shark. And even without a guide you can easily observe for yourself the confetti-hued reef fish, shoals of which are everywhere to be seen in these exceptionally temperate waters. Like its marine life, Thailand's extraordinary richness lies beneath the surface – all you have to do to discover it is dive!

11

Royal house and spirit houses

In Thailand even the king is correctly addressed by his first name.
And good manners are expected of everyone, not just spirits

Working elephants

For centuries these grey giants were put to work logging in Thailand's forests. Since 1989 however, tree felling has been prohibited throughout the country in an effort to conserve the already seriously decimated woodland, and as a result the elephants are out of work. These days they no longer haul huge hardwood tree trunks from the jungle; instead they have been redeployed to new positions in the tourist industry. They play football, sit up and beg, and suffer strangers to ride on their broad backs. For some years now, particularly on the island of Phuket in southern Thailand, *elephant trekking* has proved a major tourist innovation. And more and more frequently this former heraldic beast of old Siam can also be seen in the centre of Bangkok and other towns. There the gentle pachyderms and their mahuts wander through the streets in search of tips. For a small sum, passers-by can feed the elephants

Wat Phra That Doi Suthep near Chiang Mai is surmounted by a gilded chedi

bananas or sugar cane, and have their photos taken with them. The animal welfare organization *Friends of the Asian Elephant* estimates that today there are as few as 4,000 domesticated elephants left in the country. This compares with 1980 when numbers were still as high as 10,000.

Mountain peoples

The *chao kao*, the people of the mountains, are referred to collectively as the *hill tribes*. They arrived as migrants, settling the hitherto almost inaccessible mountainous regions of northern Thailand after having made their way across the vast intervening distances from southern China and Tibet via Laos and Burma. Today they number some 750,000 people. The largest tribe is the Karen, to which some 350,000 belong, and who occupy virtually the entire frontier region between Thailand and Myanmar (formerly Burma) right the way down to southern Thailand. The various tribes differ greatly in language and culture. Originally animists, today many have either been Christianized by missionaries or converted to Buddhism. The government builds schools in the villages in the hope of better integrating the mountain people into Thai society.

The *chao kao* engage in traditional slash and burn agriculture. The cultivation of poppies for the manufacture of opium and heroine has largely been stemmed as a result of police raids. Numerous internationally supported projects aim to provide a viable alternative by promoting the cultivation of vegetables, fruit, coffee and tea in the mountains. Tourist trekking also provides a modest source of income for many villages.

Population

Thailand today has a population of some 61.5 million. The 60 million mark was officially reached on 2 November 1996 at 9.48 pm with the birth of Poramet Boonsawat, a baby boy into whose cradle the Ministry of the Interior put a gold amulet, a grant towards his education, and the sum of Bahts 10,000. The Thai government also had some reason to celebrate, because the dire warnings of an army of demographic experts had proved unfounded. At the end of the nineteen seventies it was still being widely predicted that, by the mid nineties, the country's population would have exploded to exceed 80 million. Family planning is high on the list of the government's priorities. The one-time Health Minister Meechai in particular was responsible for disseminating information on contraception to people throughout the country.

Some 75 per cent of the population are ethnic Thais, while 14 per cent are of Chinese extraction.

A further 3.5 per cent are Muslim Malays (an ethnic group, not a nationality) living in the provinces near the Malaysian border. The rest of the population is made up of Khmer, Laotians, Vietnamese, Mon, Shan and various tribes.

Buddhism

About 95 per cent of all Thais are Buddhists. Especially in country areas, young men are still expected to spend some time as a monk in a monastery. Thais hang house-altars with statues of Buddha in their houses, and many of them wear amulets around their necks containing pictures of the Enlightened One or some particularly revered monk. Buddhism plays a much greater role in the everyday lives of the Thais than Christianity does in the case of the majority of people in the West. Thais regularly go to temples to ask Buddha to intercede for them; and they will always seek Buddha's blessing before embarking on a journey, an examination, an interview or going into hospital. Yet the established state religion is fast losing its significance, tending increasingly to ossify into mere ritual. In Buddhism life means suffering. To attain Nirvana a person must break out of the eternal cycle of birth and rebirth. Among the reasons for suffering is, for example, the desire for possessions. All of which runs counter to the ethos of the times, in which the economic boom has virtually turned striving for affluence into a new religion – to the extent that commercialism has even overtaken monks and monasteries. The young Buddhist novices who take their begging bowls from house to house in the early mornings, will nowadays also accept money, which doctrinally they are forbidden to do. And sometimes they have been known to collect more food than they strictly need and sell the surplus later. A survey sponsored by the Thai Farmers Bank revealed that 44.5 per cent of the population are now seriously disenchanted with the behaviour of the monks.

Education

Children are statutorily obliged to attend school for a minimum period of nine years. Many children, though, finish school after only six years – in some cases abandoning their studies even earlier. This is particularly true of girls in rural districts. From a very early age they are expected to help with the housework and in the fields. Nevertheless Thailand can be proud of its progressive record in education. According to the statistics, 93.8 per cent of the population are able to read and write, one of the highest literacy rates anywhere in Asia. An essential element of education in the home is the importance placed on the family. Children are taught to honour their parents, and to take responsibility for younger siblings. In a country without a state pension scheme, family cohesion is a matter of immense financial significance. It is taken for granted that children will provide and care for their parents when the latter are no longer able to fend for themselves.

Falang

Thais refer to all white-skinned foreigners as *falang*, a term which is not intended to be in any way derogatory. Simply meaning "white stranger", it is possibly a corruption of the English word foreigner. The vast majority of Thais have long since become accustomed to tourists from the West. But in remote parts of the country children seeing a foreigner may still all cry out "falang, falang" in surprise and alarm – and sometimes take to

A spirit house: every morning brings another offering or two

their heels at the sight of these strange, alien creatures.

Spirit houses

Despite the Thais' devotion to Buddhism, their world continues to be one inhabited by *phii*, or spirits. To prevent these spirits wandering about causing mischief, a house must be built to accommodate them. No matter whether it be small and of simple construction like a bird-house, or many feet tall and splendid like a temple, in Thailand nobody would dream of occupying so much as a pile-dwelling, never mind a skyscraper, until a spirit house has been erected in front of it. And every morning the invisible neighbours are presented with gifts, such as flowers, rice, a glass of water or even – on especially important days – a roast chicken.

The Thai royal house

Even though Thailand's absolute monarchy was abolished in 1932, the Thai royal house still commands the utmost respect. To insult royalty continues to be a punishable offence. During audiences even high-ranking Thais, the prime minister included, sit on the carpet at the king's feet, having approached him in a squatting position. The present head of the Chakri dynasty, King Bhumibol Adulyadej, otherwise known as Rama IX, is revered by all sections of Thai society. The monarch, who was born in the USA in 1927, ascended the throne in 1946. Through all the political turmoil of the intervening years, he has not merely retained his authority but enhanced it. Together with Queen Sirikit he has four children: Princess Ubol Ratana (born 1951), Prince Maha Vajiralongkorn (1952), Princess Maha Chakri Sirindhorn (1955) and Princess Chulabhorn (1957).

Names

Whether talking to the postman or the prime minister, Thais normally address one another by their first names, in front of which they attach *Khun*, (Mr or Mrs).

Virtually every Thai has a nickname (*chu len*, literally: playname). Animal names are very popular. It is only Westerners who are likely to be surprised if someone introduces himself quite unselfconsciously as *mu* (pig), *kob* (frog), *gung* (crab), or *gai* (chicken). In Thailand nicknames like this are not used to poke fun at people but as terms of affection. After all, it is their mothers who bestow these unofficial first names on the infant Thais in their cradles. Their real first names, by contrast, are generally speaking only used when engaged on some sort of official business or in dealings with the authorities.

Prostitution

Adult prostitution, though not the activities of pimps, was legalized in Thailand in 1997. Simultaneously a start was made on combating child abuse by introducing special protection for children under 15 years of age and drastically increasing the penalties for offenders. The number of under age prostitutes in Thailand is estimated at between 200,000 and 800,000. Many of them originate from Myanmar and southern China, there having been lured from their home villages by pimps before being smuggled over the border and forced into prostitution. It is indisputable that tourism has contributed considerably both to the spread of prostitution and to the sexual abuse of children. Many Western countries have now introduced legislation of their own making it possible to pursue offenders through their internal courts, with conviction leading to prison sentences. One of the consequences of prostitution is the spread of AIDS; according to the World Health Organisation (WHO), as many as 4 million Thai men and women are now (2000) infected with the HIV virus.

Government

In 1932 Thailand's absolute monarchy was abolished and replaced by a constitutional one, the king being head of state and supreme commander of the armed forces. Although he does not involve himself in day-to-day politics as such, it is nevertheless the case that no government can realistically expect to institute policies to which the king is opposed. His wish is still taken as a command. The government is led by an elected prime minister. Parliament consists of an elected house of representatives and an appointed Senate. A political scene such as is commonly found in the West, with opposing parties differentiated by competing ideologies, is completely alien to Thailand. Politicians frequently change allegiance from one party to another, and the setting up of new parties is by no means uncommon. Administratively the country is divided into 76 provinces, each having a governor appointed by the interior ministry.

Manners and customs

The Thais are an exceptionally tolerant people and do not attempt to interfere in the affairs of others; certainly not those of foreign tourists, who find themselves able to do much as they please. The Thai response to excessively bad behaviour on the part of visitors is a *falang bah* – the white foreigners are crazy. However there are situations which try even a Thai's patience beyond endurance – for instance if disparaging remarks are made about royalty. Likewise Buddhism, its representatives and its symbols should always be treated with respect. Shoes must be taken off when entering temples (except Chinese temples), mosques and private houses. Women are not allowed to touch monks, nor are they permitted to sit next to them on buses. Thais dress neatly and demurely when they leave their houses. Anyone who does not take care of his appearance loses face (even if he is completely unaware of it himself!). When visiting a temple or engaged in dealings with the authorities, it is essential to be neatly and tidily dressed. Otherwise you will be refused entrance, served extremely slowly, or even totally ignored. Though many tourists do indulge in it, in Thailand topless sunbathing offends against good taste. Nudism is completely unacceptable and a punishable offence. Showing anger by shouting or raising your voice infringes no law but is similarly looked down upon with scorn and disdain. Thais regard losing control of yourself as one of the least admirable of traits.

The Thais do not consider the

In Thai boxing good foot-work includes a powerful kick

head to be "sacred" as many Westerners believe; nevertheless it is, in a figurative as well as a literal sense, the highest part of the body. As a foreigner you should never touch a Thai on the head, even as a friendly gesture. In the same way, since the foot is the lowest part of the body, it should never be pointed at another person. This should be remembered at all times – even if you feel yourself getting cramp or pins and needles through sitting too long cross-legged.

Thai boxing

The national sport involves the use of bare feet as well as fists. Drummers are there to heighten the mood. It is almost as interesting to watch the enthusiasm of the spectators around the ring as the fight going on inside it. Notorious gamblers that they are, the Thais never miss an opportunity to place a bet.

Tourism

One branch of industry remained unaffected by the recent economic crisis: tourism. Quite the reverse in fact; the collapse of the country's currency further boosted this vital sector of the economy. In 1998 there were some 7.76 million foreign visitors, an increase of 7.53 per cent over the previous year. This makes Thailand the number one Asian tourist destination by a considerable margin. Though the largest visiting group (1 million) were Malaysians, many of these were only crossing the border on day trips. A further 2.1 million tourists came from Europe. The time has long since past when practically all visitors to Thailand were men. Now some 40 per cent are women, a substantial increase from 10 per cent.

Fortune tellers

No matter how good or bad the economic situation, one particular trade is always booming: fortune telling. Everyone has their fortune told – politicians too.

Even monks engage in predicting the future, which of course has nothing at all to do with Buddhism. Research carried out by the Thai Farmers Bank indicated that every year the Thais spend the equivalent of US $143 million (£95 million) on fortune tellers and books and journals on the subject. In any given year, 25 per cent of all Thais consult a fortune teller at least once; and in the case of politicians the figure is said to rise to 84 per cent.

Wai

Thais do not greet one another by shaking hands but with a *wai*. This graceful gesture is made by raising the folded hands in front of the lower half of the face. This sounds much easier than it is, because there are also a considerable number of rules to be observed. For instance the younger person makes the first *wai*, as does a person more subordinate in rank, the hands being positioned higher or lower according to the status of the other, likewise the head bowed to a corresponding degree. The highest *wai* and the deepest bow of the head are reserved for the royal family. It is perfectly in order though to greet someone with a friendly smile and a nod of the head. You should never return the *wai* of a child, servants or domestic staff, or beggars – to do so would make you look extremely foolish.

Wat

Wat is the Thai word for a temple and monastery complex. Normally temples and monasteries are found together, one exception being the *Wat Phra Keo* in the Grand Palace: this royal temple has no monastery attached to it. The prayer hall of a *wat* is called a *bot*. It is often decorated with precious murals and reliefs and always houses a statue of Buddha. In a *bot* the faithful sit or kneel on the ground. *Chedi* are towers, bell-like at the foot and tapering to a point at the top. Towers in the classical Khmer style are called *prang*. Particularly in rural areas the *wat* is not only the centre of religious but also of community life. People go there to pray and meditate, but festivities take place there too – and no amount of fairs or feasting and merry-making ever seems to distract the monks from their sacred duties.

Economy

Even though approximately half the working population of Thailand still earn their daily rice from agriculture, the industrialization of the country proceeded apace during the boom years recently past. Industrial activity is still largely concentrated however in the greater Bangkok area and on the nearby east coast.

Important export products in the agriculture sector include for example rice (Thailand is the biggest exporter in the world), pineapples, rubber, palm oil and prawns. Manufacturing industry exports principally electrical and electronic goods and accessories used in vehicle construction. In 1998 as in previous years, textiles were the main foreign currency earner – as well as being very popular with tourists, offering some of the best value for money of any souvenir from Thailand. Thailand is also a leading exporter of jewellery and gemstones.

A kingdom for gourmets

Thai cuisine is often highly spiced but always light – and desserts are a mouth-watering treat for anyone who loves fruit

Not only is Thai cuisine widely considered among the best in the world, it is also extremely digestible, so that even weeks of feasting can be indulged in without ruing the consequences. It goes without saying that in a country where people love eating chilli, many dishes are not only divinely delectable but also devilishly spicy. But if you are not among the fire-eaters there is no need to despair; you will find plenty of good things to eat which won't bring tears to your eyes.

In the tourist resorts of course, you could if so inclined embark upon a sort of world-wide culinary tour. The particular cuisine of almost every nationality represented among visiting holiday-makers is also catered for. Whether it be Spanish, American, Italian, German, Greek, Arab or Russian – the choice is simply enormous. But when there are so many wonderful local specialities on offer, it really is a sin to settle for a hamburger and chips.

Every street corner has its little snack bar, where food sizzles and steams. Itinerant street vendors sell grilled squid, kebabs or fruit cooled on ice. Mobile snack stands pull into the kerb, a few stools and a table or two are set up on the pavement, and lo and behold there is an open-air restaurant. Over a hissing gas burner or charcoal brazier a tasty meal is prepared in the flick of a wrist: noodle soup with chicken or duck, fried rice with crab, an omelette with tiny mussels, or pancakes with pineapple chunks.

Kin kao jang? – Have you eaten already? – is a very common form of greeting in Thailand; because eating several times a day, and in company whenever possible, is an important part of the Thai way of life. Red meat is used sparingly. Poultry and seafood appear on the plate more often. Vegetables are only cooked al dente, so they remain crisp and rich in vitamins. A multitude of different herbs and

Water melons are transformed into succulent works of art

21

spices give the dishes their particular flavour. For example coriander, lemon grass and lemon leaves, ginger, basil, tamarind and mint, curry and prawn paste. Not to mention garlic and chilli! The Thais consider any meal lacking at least one fiery dish to be *mai aloi*, – not tasty. The courses though are light and do not leave you with that heavy feeling – as long, that is, as you follow the Thai example and partake of a lot of little snacks all through the day and half the night, rather than one sumptuous repast. Only the better class restaurants impose set hours for lunch (usually about 11.30 am to 2 pm) and dinner (about 6 to 10 pm). Many more modest establishments continue serving until late at night, and in the bigger towns and tourist resorts, the snack stands on the streets continue in business virtually round the clock.

Thai dishes come already served in bite-sized pieces and can easily be eaten with a spoon and fork. The spoon is held in the right hand, the fork being used only to push the next mouthful onto the spoon. Chopsticks are generally only provided for noodles, and also soups, these having been introduced by the Chinese. A typical Thai bill of fare for a fairly large group of people consists of dishes with five different tastes: bitter, sweet, sour, salty and spicy. These will be accompanied by a big bowl of rice. Everyone serves himself, and it doesn't matter in which order the dishes are eaten. It is not considered polite, however, to pile everything onto your plate at once.

Though Thai food is very distinctive and unmistakable, the influence of Chinese, Indian and Malay cuisine in particular is nonetheless strong. Furthermore, there are pronounced regional variations. For example *kao niau*, sticky rice, is very much to the liking of people in the northeast, while among southern Thais *gaeng massaman*, a (rather spicy) red curry with pieces of beef, peanuts and potatoes is a particular favourite.

Gaeng kiau wan gai, a green curry with chicken and aubergines is a speciality prone to induce sweating. Not exactly a gastronomic highlight, but solid fare even so, is *kao pat*, fried rice prepared with eggs (*kai*), vegetables (*pak*), and crab (*gung*), pork (*mu*) or chicken (*gai*). The most popular snack between meals is *kui tiao nam*, a noodle soup especially tasty when made with duck (*pet*), and which, like *kao pet*, is not spicy. Something which might be regarded as Thailand's national dish is the spicy *tom yam gung*, a slightly sour prawn soup which gets its unmistakable tang from the lemon grass used to flavour it.

Another exotic dish to whet the appetite is *tom kha gai*, a very spicy soup made with chicken in coconut milk and laced with chillies. And if you are looking for a snack there is always *plamuk tohd katiam pik thai*, squid fried in garlic and pepper (not spicy).

From north-east Thailand comes *som tam*, a salad made with thin strips of green papaya, tomatoes, dried shrimps, small crabs and plenty of chillies. It is eaten with raw vegetables, sticky rice and grilled chicken (*gai pat*). The

Thais are particularly fond of seafood; unfortunately there is now very little left to be harvested in their own coastal waters. Consequently, the famous *Phuket lobster* for example, which is not actually a lobster but a langouste, now comes mainly from the fishing grounds of Myanmar.

Thais make very liberal use of chillies. In restaurants popular with tourists, where in this respect at least very little of the food continues to be prepared in the authentic way, these little trouble-makers are added more sparingly. But to be on the safe side you can always say *mai peht* (not spicy) when ordering. Basic dishes such as fried rice, fried noodles and noodle soup are served plain for guests to season for themselves, every table being laid with little pots containing dried and ground chillies, sugar (for the noodle soup) and a sweet and sour vinegar with fresh chilli pieces floating in it. You will search in vain for a salt cellar in a typical Thai restaurant. Instead you will find *nam pla*, a clear light brown liquid made from fermented fish. Mixed with finely chopped chillies the fish sauce becomes *pik nam pla* – be careful not to take too much!

Thailand is a mecca for the fructophile. Anyone who limits themselves to bananas, pineapples, water melons and papayas (the cheapest fruits) has only themselves to blame! Depending on the season, the markets are overflowing with various kinds of fruit, which at home are either exorbitantly expensive or not available at all. Thais consider *durians* or "stink fruit" the best of all. The yellowy-white pulp under the spiny shell is almost creamy in texture, and after the first bite people either crave it or never want to taste it again. There is no such divergence of opinion when it comes to mangoes (*mamuang*) however, particularly tasty when eaten with concentrated coconut milk and sticky rice. The Thais also savour green mango cut in strips, which they dunk in a mixture of sugar and chillies. Under the thick wine-red rind of the delicate mangosteen (*mangkut*) is a juicy white pulp that tastes at once sweet and slightly acidic. You should also make a definite point of trying the hairy rambutans (*ngo*), the delicately scented lychees (*lintschi*) and the java apples (*chompu*), which latter look like little bells.

When it comes to fruit juices the choice is usually limited to just orange juice – which itself is often spun out with lemonade. Bottled water (*nam bau*) and mineral water are available everywhere as thirst-quenchers. The most popular home-brewed beer is *Singha*, but it will not be to everyone's taste on account of the preservatives. Other brands of beer also brewed in Thailand include Kloster, Becks and Carlsberg. Thailand's unofficial national drink is the moderately priced *Mekhong*. Distilled from rice it is officially classed as a whisky but in reality is more like a type of rum. The Thais make a long drink of it by adding mineral water (tourists tend to favour coke) together with a good dash of lemon juice on ice.

Pearls, gold and silk

Whether in search of jewellery, beautiful lacquerwork, a new pair of spectacles or a wooden toy – shopping in Thailand is always fun

Shopping is one of Thailand's most popular leisure activities and it is not at all difficult to see why. The choice of merchandise is simply enormous. For visitors from the West there is the added attraction that prices are often astonishingly reasonable, not to mention the service which is always friendly. Needless to say, Bangkok is the shopping capital of the country, with labyrinthine markets to explore and vast shopping precincts to wander through. Street vendors offer everything from counterfeit replicas of branded watches to authentic wooden toys. Many souvenirs and most items of handicraft are made in the north of Thailand. The northern city of Chiang Mai, with its many shops and night-time bazaars bursting at the seams, is second only to Bangkok as the place to buy.

It is worth bearing in mind that, price-wise, Thailand has a great deal more to offer than just the usual run of souvenirs. A wide range of other items, including for example spectacles, proprietary medicines and spices, cost only a fraction of what you would pay at home.

In the department stores prices are fixed. Similarly, many retail outlets in shopping precincts, and shops in tourist resorts, display a price on their goods. Even so, in these sorts of places you can generally get something off with a bit of persuasion. And as for street vendors, you should always haggle. Department stores and shopping precincts are open daily from 10 am to 10 pm; in holiday resorts the hours are often even longer. Many shops – and certainly street vendors – are happy to do business late into the night.

Antiques

Antiques should only be purchased from reputable specialist dealers displaying the blue symbol of TAT, the Tourism Authority of Thailand. Another indication of reliability is if the assistant draws your attention to the need for an export

The vast selection of wares soon banishes any thought of resisting consumerism

permit, without which you may incur considerable penalties when you come to leave the country. If the shop does not provide you with an export permit for an item, you must obtain one yourself – which can be a time-consuming business. For further information contact the *Department of Fine Arts* of the National Museum of Bangkok *(Tel. 02/224 13 70)*, or the National Museum in Songkhla in southern Thailand *(Tel. 074/31 17 28)*.

Buddha figures
Non-Buddhists are forbidden to export Buddha figures irrespective of whether they are old or new. The Thais take a dim view of people wanting a Buddha simply as a souvenir. The only Buddhism-related items tourists are permitted to take out of the country are amulets to be worn on the body.

Gold and precious stones
The Thai jewellery industry has an excellent reputation. On no account though should you purchase jewellery from itinerant vendors. Only go to reputable jewellers registered with TAT (look for the blue symbol on the door).

Gold jewellery is sold in special gold shops, the largest of which are located in Bangkok's Chinatown. They are frequented almost exclusively by Thais, but as a tourist you can still be reasonably confident you will not be cheated.

Clothes
If buying from a tailor, be sure to arrange at least one fitting, and insist on alterations if necessary. It is customary to pay a deposit, but you should only hand over the balance when everything is to your satisfaction.

In Bangkok in particular there is a vast selection of ready-made garments to choose from. Though outsize clothing for Westerners may be hard to come by, the average person should have no difficulty in finding something to suit.

Lacquerwork and ceramics
Lacquerwork is a traditional craft in which wood is lacquered several times over and then painted by hand. Lacquered items are either gold-coloured on black or yellow and green on a rust-red background. The most common are small pieces of furniture, boxes, vases and figures. Ceramic work is another craft with a long tradition locally, which is why you see many pieces which replicate older designs. Among the brightest and most skillfully produced are the bencharongs with their five colours (green, blue, yellow, pink and black) and floral patterns. Most Chinese-style ceramics retain the familiar blue and white colour-scheme. In contrast, the Seladon (porcelain) from northern Thailand comes in a distinctive jade green.

Leather, skins and shells
Certain animal products, such as snake-skin belts and crocodile accessories, cannot be exported without a permit or certificate of origin. Generally speaking the export of skins of protected species such as leopards and tigers is banned. Animal conservation is undoubtedly best fostered by not buying such products at all. If you must buy a crocodile-skin purse or handbag, at least be sure to obtain a certificate of origin confirming that the skin is from a farm where crocodiles are bred. The

Paper umbrellas are painted by hand in Bor Sang near Chiang Mai

export (and also import!) of shells and corals raises similar issues. Conservationists are at pains to point out that the souvenir industry has virtually stripped Thailand's coastal waters bare and that most shells and corals now come from the Philippines.

Pearls

Cultured Thai pearls come from the island of Phuket. Here you can visit farms where these highly prized "gems" are grown within the shells of pearl-producing molluscs. You will also be given tips on how to distinguish real from artificial pearls: unlike the artificial ones, real pearls do not feel perfectly smooth and flawlessly round when put in the mouth and gently bitten.

Counterfeit goods

Traders in counterfeit goods can supply imitations of just about any expensive product bearing the name of a well-known designer or manufacturer, everything from wrist watches to T-shirts, jeans and scent. The copies often appear deceptively genuine but cost only a fraction of the price of the real thing. Naturally the manufacture and trade in counterfeit goods is illegal in Thailand as elsewhere, but the demand among tourists is simply too great. Purchasers from abroad will generally not encounter problems with the local Thai police, but the attitude of customs officials when they return home will almost certainly be less accommodating.

Silk

With its fine sheen, Thai silk is a temptation to the buyer. But beware: all that is marked "100% pure" is not necessarily 100% pure silk. Very often it is either mixed with artificial fibre or completely artificial. Since Thai silk is hand woven it is never perfectly smooth but covered with little knots.

The romantic and the traditional

The Thais are a happy people, with an eye ever open for "sanuk", or fun

The Thais never let slip an opportunity to celebrate. In short, they are a happy people, with an eye ever open for *sanuk*, that is to say, fun. In the land of smiles this enjoyment of life manifests itself in a year-round succession of colourful festivals.

Religious feasts usually fall on days when there is a full moon and consequently the date changes from year to year. Similarly, local festivals often take place at weekends and so are movable too. Tourist offices compile and publish lists of the relevant dates for the year.

The Buddhist calendar, incidentally, starts from the year of the Enlightened One's birth. In the Buddhist calendar therefore, AD 2000 corresponds to the year 2543.

PUBLIC HOLIDAYS

National and local government offices and banks, but not bureaux de change, are closed on public holidays. Nightclubs are

The Loi Kratong Festival is lavishly celebrated in Sukhothai

not normally permitted to open on religious holidays.

1 January: *New Year's Day*

Full moon in February: *Makha Pucha*, celebrating Buddha's sermon to 1,250 followers

6 April: *Chakri Day*, marking the accession to the throne of Rama I and the founding of the Chakri dynasty (1782)

12–14 April: *Songkran*, the Thai New Year festival

1 May: *Labour Day*

5 May: *Coronation Day*, anniversary of the coronation of the present monarch, King Bhumibol Adulyadej (Rama IX)

Full moon in May: *Visakha Pucha*, commemorating Buddha's birth, enlightenment and death

Full moon in July: *Asaha Pucha*, celebrates Buddha's first sermon

One day after Asaha Pucha: *Khaopansa*, start of the Buddhist fast

12 August: *Queen Sirikit's birthday*

23 October: *Chulalongkorn Day*, anniversary of the death in 1910 of King Chulalongkorn (Rama V)

5 December: *King Bhumibol's birthday*

10 December: *Constitution Day*

31 December: *New Year's Eve*

January

Bor Sang Umbrella Festival: The village of Bor Sang is famous for its hand-painted paper umbrellas. Procession and exhibition.

January/February

Chinese New Year Festival: Celebrated with a dragon and lion parade in Nakhon Sawan in central Thailand. On Phuket a week-long temple festival is held in the Chalong Monastery (*Wat*).

February

Flower Festival: Procession with extravagantly decorated floats in Chiang Mai. (Beginning of the month)

Makha Pucha: Candle-lit processions in the temples, particularly beautiful in Wat Benjamabophit (the Marble Temple).

March

Thao Suranari Festival: A festival held in Korat (north-east Thailand) in honour of the folk heroine who saved the city from the Burmese. Week-long celebration with processions, exhibitions and fair, usually the end of March.

April

Chakri Day: 6 April, the one day in the year when the public is admitted to the royal pantheon, with its statues of past kings, in the Grand Palace in Bangkok.
★ *Songkran:* The Thai New Year Festival, from 12 to 14 April (15 April in Chiang Mai), is the most high spirited of all. People douse each other with water.

May

★ *Royal Ploughing Ceremony:* Start of the rice sowing season. Superb spectacle in front of the Grand Palace in Bangkok in the presence of the king. Seats can be reserved in the stand through the tourist office in Bangkok.

During the second week in May *Rocket Festival:* Farmers in Yasothon in the north-east fire huge rockets up into the sky in the hope of ensuring rain for the rice paddies.

MARCO POLO SELECTION: FESTIVALS

1 Songkran
The most gleeful and high-spirited water fight in the world, with even adults encouraged to behave like children again (page 30)

2 Loi Kratong
An enchanting occasion for anyone in the least romantic. The water spirits are honoured with an armada of little boats (page 31)

3 Vegetarian Festival
Definitely not for the squeamish. Witnessing what human beings are capable of when in a trance is quite an experience (page 31)

4 Royal Ploughing Ceremony
Ancient rites recall the glory of courtly Siam and the significance of the rice sowing for the entire population (page 30)

June

Phi Ta Khon Festival: Spirit Festival in the province of Loei in the north-east of Thailand, usually at the end of June. Young men roam through the streets dressed up as ghosts. The festival is celebrated most splendidly in the village of Dan Sai near the chief provincial town of Loei.

July

Candle Festival: A procession of huge wax statues and carved candles held in Ubon Ratchathani in north-east Thailand.

August

Queen Sirikit's Birthday: On 12 August. Public buildings are decorated with fairy lights, national flags and portraits of the queen – the most impressive displays are along the Ratchadamnoen Road and at the Grand Palace.

September/October

Boat races: With as many as 40 oarsmen propelling each longboat. In Phichit and Phitsanulok (central Thailand), Nan (north) and Phimai (north-east)

October

Buffalo racing: In Chonburi (between Bangkok and Pattaya). The jockeys are young country lads and their mounts water buffaloes.

★ *Vegetarian Festival:* Bizarre festival on Phuket; also, on a somewhat smaller scale, in Trang (southern Thailand). Having worked themselves into a trance the (Chinese) participants pierce their flesh with prongs, needles, hooks, even handdrills and umbrellas. The festival, which honours the nine Chinese guardian spirits, is thought to have been celebrated for the first time in the mid 19th century. An itinerant Chinese theatre troupe are said to have initiated it when seeking aid from the spirits to combat a mysterious illness afflicting the actors and local people.

November

Elephant Round-up: Elephants play football and engage in trials of strength, and old battles are re-enacted. Superbly colourful event full of tradition. Mid/end of November in Surin (north-east Thailand)

★ *Loi Kratong:* The most enchanting festival of the year – little baskets carrying burning candles are set floating on the water. At its most romantic and traditional in the old royal cities of Sukhothai and Ayutthaya as well as in Chiang Mai. (Full moon in November).

November/December

River Kwai Bridge Week: The famous bridge and "Death Railway" are central to the events. Rides on old steam trains, impressive firework displays and a son et lumière show right next to the bridge in Kanchanaburi.

December

Colour Parade: Attired in splendid ceremonial uniforms, the Royal Guard parade their Colours on the Royal Plaza in front of the old Parliament Building in the Ratchadamnoen Road in Bangkok, renewing their oath of allegiance to His Majesty. (3 December)

King Bhumibol's Birthday: As on Queen Sirikit's birthday, Bangkok is ablaze with lights. (5 December)

☛ **City Map inside back cover**

(**106/C 1**) Thailand's capital (Pop. ca. 8 million) has a multitude of faces; behind its modern façade and all the trappings of the twenty-first century, the city remains thoroughly exotic. Despite "Bangkok" having gained near-universal acceptance throughout the world, the Thais themselves refer to their capital by the more picturesque name of *Krungthep*, "the city of angels". Bangkok of course has a great many fascinating sights and places of interest which every tourist should see. But the city's pulse beats elsewhere: for example in the bustle of Chinatown, where old men while away the time sipping their morning coffee in tiny bars. Or in the *Silom Road*, Bangkok's Wall Street, where during their lunch break the money men sit at wobbly tables eating noodle soup. So let yourself be carried along through the streets and alleyways of this great city which, though it might be accused of a lot of things, can never be called boring.

SIGHTS

Grand Palace and
Wat Phra Keo   (U/A 3)

Situated in the historic centre of Bangkok, the royal palace with its Temple of the Emerald Buddha is by far the most famous sight in the whole of Thailand. Awaiting the visitor behind the whitewashed, crenellated walls is an architectural ensemble of fairytale beauty. The pièce de résistance is the superlative royal temple, *Wat Phra Keo*, in which is

Temple guard in the Grand Palace

housed the legendary Emerald Buddha, the country's most revered statue of the Enlightened One. Some of the buildings making up the royal palace are in the classical Thai style, others are Victorian. Nowadays they are used only for official business, the royal family residing in the Chitralada Palace, near Dusit Zoo. Tourists are required to be correctly dressed before entering the Grand Palace. Women should wear skirts reaching at least to the knee; sleeveless tops and blouses are unsuitable. Men should wear full-length trousers. Open-backed sandals are also unacceptable. If necessary shoes and capes can be borrowed at the entrance. *Open daily 8.30–11.30 am and 1–3.30 pm, entrance Bahts 125, Na Phralan Road.* The ticket also gains the visitor admission to the *Royal Coin and Decorations Collection (in the palace precinct)* as well as to the *Vimanmek Royal Palace (Rajawithi Road)*, the largest teak-constructed palace in the world.

Klongs (U/A–B 4–6)

In the Thonburi district people and goods are still transported by water. All the travel agents arrange tours, but you can if you prefer hire a motor-boat yourself, complete with someone to steer it. The boats can be found at the landing stages on the Chao Phraya River – behind the Grand Palace for example, or by the Hotel Oriental. *Bahts 350–450 per hour (but you must haggle!)*

Sampeng Lane (U/B 4)

❂ Old Bangkok lives on in this narrow alleyway in Chinatown, little shop after little shop squeezed in together, many appearing just as they must have done 100 years ago. Not exactly a shopping mile, but totally fascinating. *Parallel to Yaowarat Road on the side nearest the Chao Phraya River*

Jim Thompson's House (U/D 3)

The American Jim Thompson almost single-handedly revived Thailand's ailing silk industry after the Second World War. In 1967 he disappeared without trace in the mountains of Malaysia. His home, seven teak houses in the classical Thai style, contains a collection of exquisitely beautiful Asiatic art and antiques. *Open Mon–Sat 9 am–4.30 pm, entrance Bahts 100, 2 Soi Kasemsan, Rama I Road*

Wat Arun (U/A 4)

◁▷ The "Temple of the Dawn", with its 79 metre-high prang, the tower richly decorated with porcelain and coloured glass, is a familiar Bangkok landmark. The climb to the top is rewarded with a superb view over the Chao Phraya and the city. *Open daily 8 am–4.30 pm, entrance Bahts 20, Arun Amarin Road, in the Thonburi district. You can cross the river easily by boat from Thien Pier near Wat Po*

Wat Benjamabophit (U/C 2)

Standing in a park surrounded by 52 statues of Buddha, this temple of Italian Carrara marble is like a brilliant white jewel. People release turtles into the canal here as votive gifts. *Open daily 9 am–5 pm, entrance Bahts 20, Sri Ayutthaya Road*

Wat Po (U/A 4)

Bangkok's oldest temple, located south of the Grand Palace, houses a huge gilded statue of the reclining Buddha, 44 m long. Note in particular the mother of pearl intarsia in the soles of the feet. A large stone phallus in the temple precinct symbolizes fertility while the many stone reliefs with scenes from the Ramayana epic are also interesting. The temple has a school of massage. *Open daily 9 am–5 pm, entrance Bahts 20, entry from Chetuphun or Thai Wang Road*

MUSEUM

National Musuem (U/A 3)

This was the residence of the viceroy, who lived here within sight of the Grand Palace. Now it offers an insight into the history, art and culture of Thailand. Exhibits range from prehistoric finds and superb ornamented howdahs to antique weapons, precious items and the royal funerary carriages. *Open Wed–Sun 9 am–4 pm, Thu 9.30 am, entrance Bahts 40, Na Phratat Road*

RESTAURANTS

All the large hotels have excellent restaurants serving food of various provenances; nor are they excessively expensive. At lunchtime in particular, even in the very best of them, it is possible to enjoy a very reasonably priced buffet. The terrace of ❀ *Ban Klang Nam (open daily from 11 am, Rama III Road, Soi 14,* **O,** *Tel. 02/292 01 75, Category 2–3)* affords a lovely view of the Chao Phraya. Thai and Chinese cuisine as well as very fine seafood. In the ❀ *Bangkok Sky Restaurant (open daily 11 am–2 pm and 6–10 pm, Ratchaprarop Road,* **U/E 3,** *Tel. 02/656 30 00, Category 2),* located in Bangkok's tallest hotel, the 309 m-high Bayoke Sky, the food is good and the view fantastic. In *Cabbages and Condoms (open daily 11.30 am–2 pm and 6–11 pm, Soi 12, Sukhumvit Road,* **F 4,** *Tel. 02/229 46 10, Category 3),* you can not only enjoy good Thai cuisine but also buy condoms – the restaurant belongs to ex-Minister of Health, Meechai, whose advocacy of birth-control was instrumental in averting a demographic crisis in the country. For the very best in Thai cuisine go to *Lemongrass (open daily 11 am–2 pm and 6–11 pm, Soi 24, Sukhumvit Road,* **O,** *Tel. 02/253 86 37, Category 1–2).* The *Nam Nak Thai (open daily from 6.30 pm, 131 Ratchadapisek Road,* **O,** *Tel. 02/276 18 10, Category 2)* is capable of seating as many as 3,000 customers (the most anywhere according to *The Guiness Book of Records);* the waiters whizz about on roller-skates and there are performances of classical Thai dancing (reserve a place near the stage). First-class *Royal Thai cuisine* beautifully presented to delight the eye as well as the palate can be found at the *Thanying (open daily from 11 am, 10 Pramuan Road, a side street off Silom Road,* **U/C 2,** *Tel. 02/236 43 61, Category 1–2;)* very elegant, very trendy.

SHOPPING

The principal shopping streets are *Sukhumvit Road* (**F 4–5**), *Silom Road* (**U/C 6–D 5**), *Rama I Road* (**U/E-F 4**) and *Ploenchit Road* (**U/F 4**). Here are found numerous department stores, shopping precincts, smaller shops and the usual multitude of street vendors. Chinatown is a shopping centre *extraordinaire* in its own right – primarily for the local community. At *Bangkok Dolls (85 Soi Ratchatapan, Ratchaprarop Road, near Pratunam Market,* **U/E 3)** there are all kinds of hand-made dolls. In the ❀ *Bo Beh Market (Krung Kasem Road,* **U/C 4)** many of the stall holders sell textiles. Here you can buy odd bits and pieces for unbelievably low prices. Just ask if you can have a sample. The ❀ *Chatuchak Weekend Market (Chatuchak Park, Kamphang Pet Road, near the northern bus station,* **O,** *Sat and Sun only)* is the biggest flea market in the country – and quite an experience. In the *Chitralada Shop (open daily 10 am–4.30 pm, Chitralada Palace, between Rama V and Sawankhalok Road, entry through the Ratwithi Gate,* **U/C 2,** *also a branch in the Grand Palace),* you can purchase craftwork and handmade items. Take some form of identification to show to the guard just in case you are asked. Skirts are obligatory for women; open sandals are not considered suitable. The ❀ *Mah Boonkrong Center (444 Phayathai Road,* **U/D 4)** has seven floors crammed with shops and stands. In ❀ *Pratunam*

Pattaya: lively tourist Mecca on the Gulf of Siam

arrangements, reasonably-priced tours can be booked through travel agents or hotels.

Mini Siam

A park with scaled-down versions of all the most famous buildings, sights etc. in Thailand and elsewhere. *Open daily 7 am–10 pm, Tel. 038/42 16 28, entrance, including transport, ca. Bahts 200*

Nong Nooch Tropical Garden

Orchids, zoo, elephant display and traditional Thai dancing. *Open daily 9 am–6 pm, shows 10.15 am, 3 and 3.45 pm, Tel. 038/42 93 21, entrance, including transport, ca. Bahts 350*

Ripley's Believe It Or Not

Proof that truth is stranger than fiction: everything from the three-legged horse to the Roman Emperor Vitelius – biggest glutton history has ever known. Located in the Royal

Garden Plaza shopping precinct (in the middle of Pattaya). *Open daily, 10 am–midnight, entrance Bahts 200*

The Million Years Stone Park & Crocodile Farm

Absolutely beautiful park with bizarre natural rock formations. Also a zoo, elephants performing tricks and a crocodile show. *Open daily, 9 am–6 pm, shows more or less hourly, Tel. 038/24 93 47, entrance, including transport, ca. Bahts 350*

RESTAURANTS

Bruno's

First-class Mediterranean and Thai cuisine served up in an elegant setting. *Open daily 6.30 pm–midnight, Sri Nakorn Center, North Pattaya, Tel. 038/36 10 73, Category 1–2*

P. I. C. Kitchen

One of Pattaya's best Thai restaurants, in traditional teak buildings. Lots of atmosphere. *Open daily 11 am–2 pm and 5.30–11 pm, Soi 5, Beach Road, Tel. 038/42 83 87, Category 2–3*

Ruen Thai Restaurant

An open-air restaurant where customers are entertained with classical Thai music and dance. *Open daily 11 am–2 pm and 6 pm–midnight, Pattaya 2 Road, South Pattaya, Tel. 038/42 59 11, Category 2*

The Mayflower

★ Dinner and live music served up on deck during an evening cruise round Pattaya Bay (afternoon trips too). *Reservations: Tel. 038/36 15 48, Bahts 650, inclusive*

Vientiane

Authentic Thai and Laotian cuisine. Many locals eat here. *Open daily 11 am–11 pm, Pattaya 2 Road, South Pattaya, Tel. 038/41 12 98, Category 3*

HOTELS

During the boom years one hotel after another was built in Pattaya. Nowadays competition for bookings here is intense and visitors can enjoy the best value for money of any Thai resort, e.g. a room costing as little as Bahts 40 a night with television, minibar and access to a pool.

Royal Garden Resort

The best hotel in the centre of the resort, with only Beach Road between it and Pattaya's principal beach. Huge swimming pool. *300 rooms, Beach Road, Tel. 038/42 81 26–7, Fax 42 99 26, Category 1*

Sea Lodge

Bungalows in attractive gardens.

Pool. Functional rooms with television and minibar. 600 m from Wong Amat Beach. *78 rooms, Soi Chavarit Thamrong, Naklua Road, Tel. 038/42 51 28, Fax 42 51 29, Category 3*

Thai Garden Resort

Highly regarded hotel. Self-catering apartments also available. Open-air and covered pools, and children's playground. Five minutes by taxi to the small, clean Wong Amat Beach, ten minutes to South Pattaya. *174 rooms, North Pattaya Road, Tel. 038/37 06 14–8, Fax 42 61 98, Category 2*

Welcome Plaza Hotel

Spacious rooms equipped with television and minibar; large pool, central location, *269 rooms, Pattaya 2 Road, Tel. 038/42 47 65–6, Fax 42 47 67, Category 3*

SPORTS & LEISURE

Golf, diving, sailing, fishing, bowling, tennis, shooting, riding, go-karting – just about everything is catered for.

ENTERTAINMENT

There is live music laid on in lots of Pattaya's bars and pubs including, for instance, the *Green Bottle Pub (adjacent to the Diana Inn Hotel, Pattaya 2 Road)* and the *Moon River Pub (in the Thai Garden Resort)*. The biggest disco is the ★ *Palladium (Pattaya 2 Road)*

Drag Shows

With their extravagant costumes and lavish sets these cabaret-style transvestite shows are truly spectacular and quite an experience:

Alcazar (Tel. 038/41 05 05) and also Tiffany's (Tel. 038/42 96 42). Both are in Pattaya 2 Road, entrance Bahts 400–600

INFORMATION

Tourism Authority of Thailand (TAT)

Here you can also pick up many brochures from private tour operators. *Open daily 8.30 am–4.30 pm, Beach Road, on Soi 8, Tel. 038/42 76 67, Fax 42 91 13*

SURROUNDING AREA

Chantaburi   (107/E 3)

☆ Climax of the day tour to the provincial capital Chantaburi, 80 km south-east of Pattaya, is a visit to the world-famous sapphire mines and an opportunity to see how precious stones are cut. Other stops generally include the hill monastery of *Wat Kao Sukim* and the waterfall in the *Pliew National Park, Cost, including lunch, about Bahts 1,000*

Elephant Village   (107/D 2)

At the Elephant Village these highly intelligent creatures are put through their paces. Afterwards there's the chance to go swaying through the Village on the back of a docile grey giant. *Pattaya Elephant Village, Mu 2 Tambon Non Prue (approximately 30 minutes from Pattaya), Tel. 038/24 98 53; the show costs about Bahts 350, elephant trekking about Bahts 700 per person*

Ko Larn   (106/C 2)

Lying barely 8 km from Pattaya, Ko Larn, only 4 sq km in area, is the most popular island for an excursion. It has white sandy beaches and clean water, but its

Demonstrating lightness of touch in Pattaya Elephant Village

In the spirit of Marco Polo

Marco Polo was the first true world traveller. He travelled with peaceful intentions forging links between the East and the West. His aim was to discover the world and explore different cultures and environments without changing or disrupting them. He is an excellent role model for the travellers of today and the future. Wherever we travel we should show respect for other peoples and the natural world.

WWF

very popularity makes for a fair amount of noise. Every day an armada of boats set off from Pattaya Bay carrying day trippers to Ko Larn. Bookings at any travel agent *(cost about Bahts 250 including lunch)*

Ko Samet (107/D 3)

Crowds of people from Bangkok like to spend a day or weekend on this island in the neighbouring province of Rayong. Ko Samet has lovely sandy beaches for bathing, but the invading hordes of trippers mean it is no longer idyllic. Longer-stay visitors (plenty of reasonably priced bungalow accommodation) are left to enjoy the peace and quiet which descends in the evenings. *Tours cost about Bahts 400, the ferry from Ban Phe fishing village Bahts 40*

KO CHANG

(107/F 4) A hilly island with summits up to 744 m, swathed in jungle; lots of little fishing villages and palm-studded beaches – and that just about sums up Ko Chang. Until the beginning of the nineties this island paradise was still only known to backpackers and accommodation meant a few bamboo huts. There were no roads and no electricity. Since then a track, now partly sur-

faced, has been cut through the jungle behind the beaches, and a submarine cable brings power from the nearby mainland. Bungalow resorts, most of them very simple, have sprung up like mushrooms after warm rain. But nothing has been built above the level of the palms and this is still a place where you feel a real sense of release. The best beach, *Hat Sai Khao* (White Sand Beach), is also the most developed. At *Klong Phrao Beach* and *Kai Bae Beach* the water is very shallow and you have to wade out quite a distance to swim. From Pattaya the easiest way to get to Ko Chang is by minibus (about Bahts 400). Buses depart hourly from the *Eastern Bus Terminal* in Bangkok to the provincial capital *Trat* (315 km, four hours). From there it is 30 minutes by *songthaeo* (public minibus) to the pier in the little port of *Laem Ngob*. Ferries leave around midday and in the early afternoon *(about Bahts 50)*.

SIGHTS

Nature lovers can rejoice; there's still not a single man-made attraction on the island. There are, though, boat trips to other islands – Ko Chang is encircled by a marine National Park with a total of 51 small isles. On Ko Chang itself there are numerous jungle waterfalls where wilting walkers can refresh themselves. The most beautiful is *Tan Mayom*, a triple-tiered falls on the island's east coast, not far from the National Park HQ (there are no pretty beaches there however). *Klong Plu* waterfall, in the centre of the island behind Klong Phrao Beach, also cascades down in three stages. Be sure to make a detour if you are doing the walk from *White Sand Beach* along ★ more deserted beaches to *Kai Bae Beach*. The walk, at first following the island road, takes several hours.

RESTAURANTS

All the resorts cater for simple meals. The Thai food at *Alina's* Resort at White Sand Beach deserves special mention. Here in the evenings, mats are rolled out on the beach and tables and chairs set up, and you can enjoy freshly grilled fish.

HOTELS

Banphu Ko Chang Hotel
This is like a South Sea Islands dream: palm-thatched, air-conditioned bungalows (with television and minibar) on White Sand Beach. There is even a small pool. *7 rooms, Tel. 039/51 24 00, Fax 54 23 59, Category 1*

Klong Phrao Resort
Bungalows with air-conditioning, fan and television on a spacious site bordering a lagoon close to the Beach. *72 rooms, Tel. 01/219 38 99, Category 2–3*

Pla Loma Cliff Resort
On a rocky point at the southern end of White Sand Beach, two minutes walk from the sandy beach. Rooms with air-conditioning, television, minibar or fan, in a lovely garden setting. Superlative view from the chalets built high on the cliffs. Also bamboo bungalows. *60 rooms, Tel. 01/219 38 80, Category 2–3*

Sea View Resort
★ The most attractive resort on the narrow Kai Bae Beach. Hillside bungalows with air-conditioning or fan. *46 rooms, Tel./Fax 01/218 50 55, Category 2–3*

White Sand Beach Resort
★ Bungalows ranging from simple to very basic set in a palm grove at the north end of the beach. The last few hundred metres must be made on foot. *37 rooms, Tel. 01/218 75 26, Category 3*

SPORTS & LEISURE

Canoes and surf-boards can be hired on White Sand Beach. Snorkelling trips to the nearby islands are organised by *Island Hopper Tour (Tel. 01/219 33 69),* also at White Sand Beach.

ENTERTAINMENT

★ Limited to one or two fun ★ beach bars on *White Sand Beach* – closing time is when the last guests leave. A myriad fairy lights strung in long chains from the bushes and palms help create an atmosphere. Fire juggling at the aptly named *Fire Bar.*

INFORMATION

Tourism Authority of Thailand (TAT)
There is a TAT office in Laem Ngob, on the left opposite the pier. *Tel./Fax 039/59 72 55*

Ancient royal cities and the bridge over the Kwai

From the cradle of Siam to the wild border country of Three Pagodas Pass

Liberally watered by the Chao Phraya River and its tributaries, the broad plain to the north of Bangkok is the country's principal rice-growing area. Here paddy fields stretch to the horizon, the young rice shoots staining the landscape a succulent green. This area, where an abundant source of food could be virtually guaranteed, was the cradle of the kingdom of Siam. In Sukhothai, where geographical speaking Thailand's north begins, the hour of the nation's birth was rung in 1238 with the founding of the first royal capital. If you get up early on a dew-spangled morning, and make your way to the Sukhothai Historical Park as the rising sun casts its gentle light over the Buddhas, columns, chedis and prangs, you will come to understand why Sukhothai bears the name "Dawn of Luck". Its luck, though, was not to last, and today Old Sukhothai is nothing more than a vast field of ruins, silent testimony in stone to

Wat Mahatat in Sukhothai: Buddha looks towards the east

a magnificent past. Ayutthaya too, the second royal city, was likewise forced to acknowledge the truth of Buddha's words: "there is no permanence on this earth". Unlike Sukhothai though, which was abandoned by its inhabitants and decayed, Ayutthaya was laid waste by the Burmese. But so massive was the scale on which Ayutthaya was built, the invaders could not level it to the ground. No matter how many heads they struck off the statues of Buddha, the temple precincts were too vast to raze. And unlike Sukhothai, Ayutthaya was not left a ghost town and rebuilt near by. Instead the threads of life were soon picked up again amidst the ruins, so that today historic Ayutthaya lies right in the heart of a busy provincial town.

To the west of Bangkok, in Kanchanaburi province, the landscape is utterly different. Having driven past sugar cane plantations, tapioca fields and uncultivated land, soon jungle-clad hills and mountain chains can be seen rising ahead. Approaching the frontier with Myanmar the country is harsh and rugged and only sparsely settled. Here yet another chapter of history waits to be re-opened, albeit one from the more recent past. The notorious bridge over the Kwai, and the infamous "Death Railway", together recall the horrors of the Second World War.

AYUTTHAYA

(103/D 5) ★ The *Chao Phraya*, *Pasak* and *Lopburi* rivers flow round the historic centre of the city (Pop. 40,000), turning it into an island approximately 3 km long and 1.5 km wide. It is dotted with the ruins of temples and palaces, whose columns and towers, rising like so many accusing fingers, dominate the skyline.

Ayutthaya being situated only 76 km from Bangkok, most visitors go there on day trips. It can be reached from Bangkok by bus (half-hourly service from the Northern Bus Terminal, *Pahonyothin Road*), by rail (hourly service) and by comfortable excursion boat (the *Oriental Queen* and the *Ayutthaya Princess* are top-class).

Arranged bus tours cost about Bahts 900. On combined bus and boat tours (about Bahts 1,900) you travel one way by bus and the other by boat. If possible you should make the return journey by boat, thereby being greeted by a Bangkok bathed in gentle evening sunlight. Whatever type of day trip you choose though, you are almost certain to run out of time. A few hours are simply not enough in which to do justice to this ancient city, even if you restrict yourself to the major sights. So anyone with an interest in history may well decide that, included as it is on UNESCO's list of World Cultural Heritage Sites, Ayutthaya with its outstanding architectural monuments, warrants an overnight stay.

SIGHTS

Ancient Palace
The royal palace was situated on the north-west edge of the city close to the walls. Like the *Grand Palace* in Bangkok, it boasted its own royal temple (*Wat Phra Si Sanphet*), the three large restored

MARCO POLO SELECTION: CENTRAL THAILAND

chedis of which are emblematic of Ayutthaya. *Open daily, 8.30 am–4.30 pm, entrance Bahts 30*

Chankasem Palace

The Burmese destroyed this palace too. But in the 19th century King Mongkut rebuilt it to use as his residence when visiting Ayutthaya. On display are statues of Buddha, old weapons, Chinese porcelain and an assortment of items from the royal household. Next to the palace stands a four-storeyed tower, the *Phisai Sanyalak*, from which the king, a keen amateur astronomer, used to observe the stars. *Wed–Sun 9 am–midday, 1–4 pm, entrance Bahts 30*

Wat Mahatat

This temple complex, at the east end of Phraram Park in the middle of what was the nucleus of the old city, is impressive on account of its vast size. As you make your way round the temple walls, keep a look out for the great banyan tree in whose roots the stone head of a decapitated Buddha has become enmeshed. *Open daily 8 am–4.30 pm, entrance Bahts 30.* No charge during the evening, when the whole complex looks even more majestic under floodlights.

Wat Panang Choen

This temple in the south-east of the city, at the confluence of the Pasak and Chao Phraya Rivers, was already standing in the mid 14th century when Ayutthaya was first founded. Its 19 metre-high statue of Buddha is said to have been completed in the year 1325.

Wat Pukao Tong

Situated some 2 km north-west

Deeply rooted: head of a Buddha in Wat Mahatat

of the island on which the old city stands, this temple is dominated by a chedi 80 metres high. Few tourists venture out as far as this and the place is an oasis of peace.

MUSEUMS

Ayutthaya Historical Study Center

The whole of the city's history and the lives of its kings and their subjects is documented here in considerable detail and in a way that is easy to take in. *Open daily 9 am–4.30 pm, entrance Bahts 100, Rotchana Road, south of Phraram Park*

Chao Sam Phraya National Museum

This museum is similarly dedicated to Ayutthaya's ancient glories. But the presentation does not match that of the neighbouring Study Center, which is much more graphic and informative. *Open daily Wed–Sun 9 am–midday, 1–4 pm, entrance Bahts 20*

There are plenty of stands serving food at the ✪ *night bazaar near the Chankasem Palace.*

Pae Krungkhao
Terrace restaurant by the Pasak River. Good seafood and Thai cuisine. *U Thong Road, Tel. 035/24 15 55, Category 3*

Ruan Doem
One of four floating restaurants near the Pridi Damron Bridge on the Pasak River. Thai cooking without frills. *U Thong Road, Tel. 035/24 19 78, Category 3*

Krung Si River
The best hotel here; on the Pasak, conveniently close to the railway station. Pool. *202 rooms, Rotchana Road, Tel. 035/24 43 33, Fax 24 37 77, Category 2*

Si Samai
Simple rooms with fan or air-conditioning; the best accommodation to be had within the historic centre. *78 rooms, 12 Thesaban Road, Tel. 035/25 22 49-50, Fax 25 16 61, Category 3*

Tourism Authority of Thailand (TAT)
Brochures etc. from the office next to the Chao Sam Phraya National Museum. *Open daily 8.30 am–4.30 pm, Si Sanphet Road, Tel. 035/24 60 76*

Bang Pa In   (103/D 6)
Royal summer palace with the magical *Aisawan Thippaya*, a water pavilion in the classical Thai style on an eyot in the Chao Phraya River. 18 km south of Ayutthaya. An obligatory stop on every organized tour. Alternatively, for about Bahts 800, you can hire a motor boat at the *Pasak pier* in Ayutthaya (near the *U Thong Hotel*), or you can take a minibus, These depart from the *Chao Prom Market* as soon as there are enough passengers. *Open daily 8.30 am–4.30 pm, entrance Bahts 50*

Bang Sai   (103/D 6)
Situated on a bend of the river near the village of Bang Sai, 15 km south of Bang Pa In, is the *Royal Folk Arts and Crafts Center.* Pottery, silk fabrics, woven baskets, pieces of furniture and carvings, are on sale. The Center can be reached by hire boat or minibus from Ayutthaya or Bang Pa In. *Open daily except Mondays 8.30 am–4 pm*

Lopburi   (103/D–E 5)
In the 10th century this provincial capital, 77 km north of Ayutthaya, was already the capital of a Khmer empire. In the 17th century King Narai made Lopburi his second city. The ruins of temple- and palace complexes from both periods are preserved in the old city centre, some of the ruins being taken over by colonies of monkeys, whom visitors feed. The huge prangs, symbolizing the Hindu trinity of Brahma (the creator), Vishnu (the preserver) and Shiva (the destroyer), form highly distinctive landmarks. Lopburi, which today has a population of 40,000, can be reached easily from Ayutthaya or Bangkok by bus or train.

KANCHANABURI

(102/C 2) The bridge over the Kwai is without question the best known structure in the whole of Thailand. Of course the iron and concrete fabrication across which you can walk, and in front of which people who have made the day trip from Bangkok often stand gaping in disappointment, in no way resembles the timber and bamboo bridge of the classic film – which in any case was not made here on the Kwai but in Sri Lanka. But if you are not yourself on a flying visit nor governed by any tour guide's rigid itinerary, you will soon discover that this border province, with its many caves and waterfalls in the jungle, has plenty to offer in the way of holiday adventure. Buses run throughout the day from Bangkok's *Southern Bus Terminal* heading for this quiet provincial capital of 40,000 people, a journey of some 130 km which takes about two hours. The train, which leaves from *Bangkok Noi Railway Station* in Thonburi, takes an hour longer (departure times are 7.50 am and 1.45 pm, but call *02/223 00 10* or *02/223 70 10* to check). The train makes a short stop at the bridge before continuing on to *Nam Tok*, where the line ends. You can board it for these final 70 km, so getting on where ★ the truly spectacular part of the journey begins. Wending its way high above the valley of the Kwai, the train passes within a whisker of sheer precipices before slowing to walking pace as it crosses a creaking timber-framed viaduct near the small town of *Wang Po.* Nam Tok, is just a sleepy little spot. You can make the return journey by train or bus; or you could continue beyond Nam Tok, up through the *Sai Yok National Park* to *Sangklaburi* near the border with Myanmar. Since this area is still new territory as far as tourists are concerned, enquire at the TAT office in Kanchanaburi before setting off.

SIGHTS

Cemeteries **(102/C 6)**
Some 6,982 allied prisoners of war were buried in the *Kan-*

Waterfall on the Kwai River in Kanchanaburi province

chanaburi *War Cemetery* situated between the town and the bridge 6 km away. The *Chung Kai War Cemetery*, on the banks of the Kwai 2 km south of the provincial capital, contains another 1,750 graves. You can hire a boat at the bridge to take you there. The trip can be combined with a visit to the *Tham Khao Poon Monastery* and stalactitic caves.

MUSEUMS

JEATH War Museum
This little museum housed in reconstructions of the camp huts in which the prisoners of war were held, was set up by the monks of *Wat Chaichumphon*. On display are old photographs, affecting pictures painted by the inmates, rusty weapons and tools. *Open daily 8.30 am–6 pm, entrance Bahts 20, Pak Phreak Road*

World War II Museum
This museum, just before the bridge, is newer and bigger. The collection is haphazard, ranging from graphic scenes showing the building of the railway to a portrait gallery of former Thai beauty queens and prehistoric finds. *Open daily 9 am–6 pm, entrance Bahts 30*

RESTAURANTS

Floating Restaurant
Authentic Thai food served aboard a raft moored above the bridge. Plenty of local colour and atmosphere. *Tel. 034/51 28 42, Category 3*

Punee Bar & Café
Located in a side street opposite the River Kwai Hotel in the town. In addition to the simple Thai and Western-style meals served here, the owner Danny Simpson keeps a supply of informative leaflets and also bicycles. *Ban Nuer Road, Tel. 034/51 35 03, Category 3*

HOTELS

If planning a weekend visit, book well in advance, because much of the hotel and raft house accommodation is taken by package tours. Arrangements can be made through any travel agent in Bangkok.

Bamboo House
The raft houses moored 300 m below the bridge offer spartan accommodation, but the gurgling water lulls you to sleep. Some rooms available with fans or air-conditioning. Pleasant garden, indeed a pleasant location altogether. *12 rooms, Soi Vietnam, Tel. 034/62 44 70 or 51 25 32, Category 3*

Felix River Kwai Resort
This resort hotel offers luxury accommodation in a riverside setting 100 metres or so above the bridge. *255 rooms, Tambun Tha Makham, Tel. 034/51 50 61-83, Fax 51 50 95, Category 1*

River Kwai Hotel
A good, middle of the range hotel. Reductions available during the week represent exceptionally good value. *161 rooms, 248 Saeng Chuto Road, Tel. 034/51 11 84, Fax 51 12 69, Category 2*

INFORMATION

R. S. P. Jumbo Travel Center
This travel agency organizes

tours with a difference, such as jungle trekking, as well as directing you to the most impressive caves and waterfalls. They will also arrange a hire car for an excursion to Three Pagodas Pass. The proprietor, Miss Chatupornpaisan ("Jumbo"), can advise in competent English. *271/3 Saeng Chuto Road, Tel. 034/51 22 80*

Tourism Authority of Thailand (TAT)

Lots of information about the whole province. *Saeng Chuto Road, Tel./Fax 034/51 12 00, open daily 8.30 am–4.30 pm*

SURROUNDING AREA

Sangklaburi (102/A 4)

★ The last town before the Burmese border, Sangklaburi (Pop. 10,000) is on the *Khao Laem* reservoir, beneath which the old Sangklaburi lies submerged with only the top of its temple still visible. The *Burmese Inn (Tambun Nong Lu, Tel./Fax*

034/59 51 46, Category 3) run by Armin Hermann and his wife Meo. Accommodation is in simple bungalows with or without their own shower. Armin has a boat and organizes tours.

There are several interesting things to see, including the extraordinary *Wang Wiwekaram* temple complex, a colourful amalgam of Indian, Burmese and Thai. The longest timber bridge in the country spans a 200 m wide branch of the reservoir to the Mon village of ✪ *Waeng Khan.* On the border, on the Thai side of the famous *Three Pagodas Pass*, 30 km north, three very weathered chedis rise starkly in the barren landscape. In Myanmar there are repeated clashes between rebels and government forces. When the situation is quiet tourists are permitted to cross the frontier (a charge of Bahts 150 is levied), but must not stray from the little market town of *Payathonzu.*

Mon village on the Khao Laem reservoir in Sangklaburi

SUKHOTHAI

(**102/C 1**) Old Sukhothai is a historical park covering an area of about 70 sq km, over which lie scattered almost 200 ruins. However, at 6 sq km the ancient centre of the first Thai capital, with 35 more or less well preserved monuments, is quite compact. The historical park is situated 12 km from new Sukhothai (Pop. 25,000). Several buses a day depart from Bangkok's *Northern Bus Terminal* for this pleasant provincial capital, 427 km to the north. The nearest rail connection is 50 km from Sukhothai at *Phitsanulok*. The *Bangkok Airways* flight from Bangkok to Chiang Mai makes a scheduled stop in the old Thai capital.

Though Sukhothai is by far the country's most important historic site after Ayutthaya, visiting tourists, of whom there tend not to be that many, are sometimes nevertheless disappointed. The ruins here do not have the monumental proportions of those in Ayutthaya and bear no comparison at all to the colossal remains at Angkor Wat in Cambodia. And even though the rulers of Sukhothai took over stylistic features from Khmer architecture, they clearly had no wish to imitate their Kmer predecessors by according themselves god-like status. Hence their buildings had a simplicity and filigree-like lightness, more in keeping with Buddhism.

SIGHTS

Historical park

★The largest and most import-ant structure in the central zone is *Wat Mahatat*, dominated by a fine chedi erected on a base decorated with reliefs; there are also rows of columns and a large number of statues of Buddha, many of which have been restored. Near by stands *Wat Si Sawai*, with three prangs. Just beyond the perimeter of the once-walled city, the chedi of *Wat Phra Phai Luang* can be seen on an island in an artificial lake. Close by, within the high walls and winged wooden gates of *Wat Si Chum*, is an 11 m-high seated Buddha, the largest such figure to survive here. The temples in this central zone are easily explored on foot. The more distant ruins can be reached with a bicycle (for hire on the approach road) or by motorcycle rickshaw. *Entrance Bahts 20 during official opening hours (6 am–6 pm), otherwise free. At temples away from the central zone you have to pay an additional charge of Bahts 10–20.*

MUSEUM

Ramkhamhaeng National Museum

The museum contains many Buddha figures and other exhibits from the Sukhothai period. The most valuable items are only replicated here, the originals having been removed to the safety of Bangkok. *Open Wed–Sun 9 am–4 pm, entrance Bahts 10, at the park entrance*

RESTAURANTS

There are some food stands at

the park entrance; but the best place to eat near the park is the *Thai Village Hotel*.

In new Sukhothai, the ☺ *night bazaar in Ramkhamhaeng Road* offers a rich selection of tasty dishes. *J.R.* in the indoor market on the same street has menus in different languages.

Dream Café

Crammed full with antiques and curiosities, this restaurant in new Sukhothai could almost be mistaken for a museum. The Thai food is excellent, as is the *Chinese fondue*, but you would be well advised to give the Western-style menu a miss. *Singhawat Road, near the Sawatipong Hotel, Tel. 055/612 08, Category 3*

HOTELS

Lotus Village

♂ A former French cultural attaché in Bangkok, and his Thai wife, run this resort on the edge of new Sukhothai's town centre. The resort, with its wooden houses, is a favourite with tourists. The accommodation is basic, ranging from simple to spartan (only one room has air-conditioning), but you enjoy a roof over your head for as little as Bahts 110 a night. Bicycle hire and tours (for instance to Si Satchanalai). *25 rooms, 170 Ratchanee Road, Tel. 055/62 14 84, Fax 62 14 63, Category 3*

River View

Best hotel in the centre; on the Yom River, near the night bazaar. Simple but with air-con-ditioning and television. *47 rooms, Nikon Kasem Road, Tel. 055/61 16 56, Fax 61 33 73, Category 3*

Thai Village Hotel

Favoured by visiting tour groups. Attractively landscaped gardens, comfortable rooms (with air-conditioning or fan) in wooden buildings, and a waterside open-air restaurant. *100 rooms, 214 Jarodvithitong Road (1 km before the park), Tel. 055/61 10 49, Fax 61 25 83, Category 3*

SURROUNDING AREA

Si Satchanalai (99/D 6)

Another historical park with temple ruins from the Sukhothai period, some 55 km north of new Sukhothai. A car with driver for the excursion costs about Bahts 800. En route, in the village of *Sawankhalok*, you can visit the *Sawan Khawaranayok National Museum (open Wed–Sun 9 am–4 pm, entrance Bahts 10)* with Buddha figures and Sawankhalok ceramic work from the Sukhothai period. Old Si Satchanalai was once walled, and had a one-time royal residence. From ☟ *Wat Khao Phanom Phloeng*, perched on a hill, some chedis can be seen rising out of the forest. 4 km north of Si Satchanalai is the *Center for Study and Preservation of Sawankhalok Kiln (open daily 9 am–4 pm, entrance Bahts 30)*. This little ceramics museum in the village of *Ban Ko Noi*, is built over ancient kilns, which have been excavated and restored.

Adventure and tribal culture

The temple city of Chiang Mai and the land of the chao kao

Of all the places away from the coast, the north is the most popular holiday destination, not just among foreign tourists but Thais as well. The mountains, with summits up to 2,565 m, can be refreshingly cool – during the winter months that is; even here summer temperatures in the valleys and towns can climb to 40°C. Overseas visitors find the ethnic variety of the region especially fascinating. Here you can roam almost at will along narrow paths to out of the way villages in which hill people, the *chao kao*, whose forebears migrated long ago from southern China, still live according to the traditions of their forefathers. Of course today the modern world reaches to even the remotest mountain hamlet. In recent decades the government has constructed many roads and brought electricity to small communities. Only as short a time ago as the nineteen seventies, the north's principal city Chiang Mai was still little more than a sleepy

With over 300 temples Buddha is everywhere in Chiang Mai

provincial town. But for all that accessibility is vastly improved, in the rugged western section of the high north, along the sparsely populated Thai-Myanmar frontier, narcotics smuggling is apparently as rife as ever.

CHIANG MAI

(**98/C 3**) The largest town in the region, Chiang Mai (Pop. 170,000), lies in the broad, fertile valley of the Ping River. Founded in 1296, it was the capital of the independent kingdom of Lanna (1296–1558). The tourist infrastructure is first class, for which reason Chiang Mai is one of the main starting points for exploring Thailand's north. There are also excellent connections by plane, rail and bus with Bangkok, 700 km away.

SIGHTS

Old City

★ Enclosed by its moat and a largely preserved brick wall, the Old City has retained much of its charm. Walking through it, every few hundred yards brings another delightful temple. Although the

86 metre-high chedi of *Wat Chedi Luang (Phrappoklao Road)* was partially destroyed by an earthquake in 1545, the 42 metres remaining, now restored, are still awe-inspiring. Worth seeing too on account of the exquisite carvings, wall paintings and elephant sculptures at the base of its chedi, is *Wat Chiang Man (Ratchapakinat Road)*, which dates from the city's foundation. A third temple, *Wat Phra Sing (Sam Lan/Sigharat Road)*, is particularly graceful. It boasts an unusual library, a masterpiece of architecture in wood.

Wat Jet Yot

This temple with its seven chedis was built in the style of the Indian Mahabodi Temple of Bodhgaya, where Buddha first attained enlightenment. *On the Superhighway, near the National Museum*

MUSEUMS

Hill Tribe Museum

The *Hill Tribe Museum* documents the history, culture and way of life of the various hill peoples. Originally housed in the university's *Tribal Research Institute*, in 1998 the museum moved to a three-storeyed, pagoda-style building on a little lakeside promontory in *Ratchamangkla Park. Open daily 9 am–4 pm, entrance Bahts 20, Chotana Road, 5 km north-west of the Old City*

National Museum

An eclectic collection: statues of Buddha as well as craftwork and assorted everyday objects. *Open Wed–Sun 9 am–4 pm, entrance Bahts 10, Superhighway, 3 km north-west of the Old City*

RESTAURANTS

There are a plethora of food stands in the *Galare Food Center* (folk dancing in the evenings) opposite the night bazaar; also in ❖ *Anusarn Market*, 300 metres further south and considerabky less touristy.

Antique House

Good Thai cooking in a truly beautiful timber house filled with antiques. *Open daily 11 am–midnight, Charoenprathet Road, Tel. 053/27 68 10, Category 3*

Ban Suan Sri Chiang Mai

A stylish, timber restaurant with excellent Thai cuisine. Situated behind *Wat Buak Krok*, on the way to Bor Sang, where the umbrellas are made. About 1½ km beyond the junction with the Superhighway, turn right down a side-road off *Sankampaeng Road*, keeping an eye open for a little sign on the right. *Open daily 11 am–10 pm, Tel. 053/26 25 68, Category 3*

The Gallery

Gallery (local artists) and restaurant in one. The attractive terrace overlooks the Ping River. *Open daily 11 am–midnight, Charoenrat Road, Tel. 053/24 86 01, Category 3*

The Riverside

❖♨ In the evenings two bands provide live music in this terrace restaurant on the Ping. Meals are also served on the *Riverside* excursion boat, which sets off every evening at 8 pm for an hour-long river trip. The restaurant is open *daily from 10 am to 1 am (Charoenrat Road, Tel. 053/24 32 39, Category 3)*.

MARCO POLO SELECTION: THE NORTH

1 Trekking
On foot through the mountains, and the villages of the hill people (page 58)

2 Raft trip on the Kok
Down the Kok River by bamboo raft from Thaton to Chiang Rai (page 61)

3 Mae Hong Son
The provincial capital of Thailand's "Siberia" makes an ideal starting point for adventure tours (page 61)

4 City of temples
A treasure-house of temple architecture: inside the old walled city of Chiang Mai (page 55)

5 Mae Sai
Over the bridge and frontier to market in Burmese Tachilek (page 63)

6 Doi Inthanon
A walk through misty forest on Thailand's highest mountain (page 58)

SHOPPING

There are surely enough handicrafts and handmade items of every kind available here to gratify even the most insatiable appetite for shopping, in particular at the night bazaar on *Chang Klan Road*. There are also numerous shops in *Tapae Road*.

In *Bor Sang* the villagers paint paper umbrellas in attractive colours. *Samkampaeng Road* on the way there is lined on both sides with little workshops etc. offering carvings, jewellery, silk and all sorts of souvenirs.

HOTELS

Compared with other Thai holiday destinations, the hotels here are extremely good value. Many guest houses tout for custom at the railway and bus stations – don't be swayed; consider all the options.

Diamond Riverside
Comfortable rooms, pool, and riverside location near the night bazaar. Excellent value for the money. *312 rooms, Charoenprathet Road, Tel. 053/27 00 80–5, Fax 27 14 82, Category 3*

Gap's House
♁ A really friendly welcome awaits at this guest house in the heart of the Old City. Air-conditioned rooms in old teak dwelling houses. *16 rooms, Soi 4, Ratchadamnoen Road, Tel. 053/27 81 40, Category 3*

River Ping Palace
Although the name has changed – it used to be called *Once upon a time* – this is still a place for romantics. An old wooden house and antique (well, almost) furniture. A little bit out of the way, about 3 km south of the night bazaar, near the Ping. *10 rooms, 385 Charoenprathet Road, Tel. 053/27 49 32, Fax 27 16 47, Category 2–3*

River View Lodge

Pleasant atmosphere, nice air-conditioned rooms with minibar and television on request. Small pool. Garden by the river. *36 rooms, Soi 2 Charoenprathet Road, Tel. 053/27 11 09, Fax 27 90 19, Category 2*

Royal Princess

The best; excellent facilities and central, by the night bazaar. *200 rooms, Changklan Road, Tel. 053/28 10 33, Fax 28 10 44, www.royalprincess.com, Category 1–2*

ENTERTAINMENT

Small cluster of bars in the upper part of *Loi Kro Road*, closest to the Old City.

Khantoke dinners (about Bahts 200), complete with displays of folk dancing, are put on virtually everywhere. Guests sit on the floor, the food is seldom special, and the whole thing is rather touristy, but it can still be fun in a group. There are discos in the larger hotels, e.g. the *Chiang Inn, Royal Princess, Porn Ping Tower and Westin.*

TREKKING

★ *Chiang Mai* is the base for most trekking tours. But since the city is not actually situated in the mountains, a drive of several hours usually precedes any walking. The alternative is to arrange to stay nearer where you plan to trek, for example in *Mae Hong Son, Mae Sai, Thaton* or *Chiang Rai*. You can pretty much take it for granted that, on one of the run-of-the-mill tours leaving from Chiang Mai and sleeping over for just two nights, you are not going to be taken to any as yet "undeveloped" area. So, wherever you're heading, be prepared to find a large number of other tourists milling about there too.

INFORMATION

Tourism Authority of Thailand (TAT)

Among the available information is a list of registered trekking agencies. *Open daily 8.30 am–4.30 pm, Chiang Mai-Lamphun Road (south of Nawarat Bridge), Tel. 053/24 86 04, Fax 24 86 05*

Internet

www.northernthailand.com, www.chiangmai-online.com

SURROUNDING AREA

The tour operators organize day trips to many different places. If you want to be independent a hire car with driver costs anything from Bahts 1,300 to 1,500 a day.

Doi Inthanon   (98/B 4)

★ A road ascends to the summit of Doi Inthanon, at 2,565 m Thailand's highest mountain. Visiting the Doi Inthanon National Park, detours can be made to several scenic waterfalls and a hill tribe village. Up on the summit are a temple, a radar station and a short track through the mist-shrouded forest. Don't forget to take a jacket or pullover! *Tour about Bahts 900, 90 km south-west of Chiang Mai*

Lamphun   (98/C 4)

Today Lamphun is just a quiet small town. Until 1281 though, it was the capital of the independent kingdom of Haripunchai. Lamphun's most celebrated sight is *Wat That Haripunchai* with its gilded 50 metre-high chedi. *26 km south of Chiang Mai. Plenty of regular buses*

Mae Sa Valley (98/C 3)

In this valley, orchid gardens, caves, snakes, butterflies, a waterfall and camps where elephants are trained follow one another in quick succession. Although inevitably a bit touristy, it is still very varied and thoroughly worth seeing. *Tour about Bahts 350, 25 km north-west of Chiang Mai*

Wat Phra That
Doi Suthep (98/C 3)

This temple on Doi Suthep (1,675 m) is famous throughout Thailand and a very popular place of pilgrimage. 3 km away stands *Phunping Palace*, the royal winter palace (viewing restricted to Fridays, Saturdays and Sundays when the royal family are not in residence). The Mon village near by is virtually lost to sight, submerged beneath a welter of souvenir shops. *Tour about Bahts 350, 15 km north-west of Chiang Mai*

CHIANG RAI

(99/D-E 1-2) Chief town of the province of the same name, Chiang Rai was founded in 1262. Today, with a population of 45,000, it is the economic hub of Thailand's far north. Even so, it preserves an attractive air of tranquility when compared with Chiang Mai. On the stroke of six in the evening the national anthem resounds over public loudspeakers. *180 km north-east of Chiang Mai, reached from there by plane or bus*

SIGHTS

One particularly delightful temple to visit is *Wat Phra Keo (Traiat Road)* which at one time housed the famous jade Buddha. Now the nation's most sacred object, the Buddha has long since been installed in the Emerald Temple in Bangkok. Also well worth seeing, close by, are *Wat Phra Sing* and *Wat Mung Muang*, the latter with a colourful morning bazaar. There is a lovely view of the town and the Kok River from *Wat Doi Tung*, on a hill on the north-western edge of the town.

MUSEUM

Tribal Museum

The *Hill Tribe Museum* maintained by the *Population & Community Development Association* provides an insight into patterns of life among the various tribes; it also organizes trekking. *Open daily 8.30 am–5 pm, Thanalai Road, Tel. 053/74 07 84, Fax 71 88 69*

RESTAURANTS

Plenty of food stands at the ☻ night bazaar in the town centre. The café at the *Golden Triangle Inn (Category 3)* has live music on Friday and Saturday evenings. Authentic Thai cuisine is also served in *Cabbages & Condoms (Category 3)* at the *Hill Tribe Museum*.

SHOPPING

The ☻ night bazaar is not on the same scale as the one in Chiang Mai. That said, handicrafts etc. made by the hill tribes can be purchased more cheaply here. And there is folk music and dancing.

Akka women show off their magnificent headresses

HOTELS

Dusit Island Resort

A luxury hotel on an island in the Kok River. When there are no tourist groups booked in, it can feel rather deserted though. *271 rooms, Kraisorasit Road, Tel. 053/71 57 77-9, Fax 71 58 01, www.dusit.com, Category L–1*

Golden Triangle Inn

Simple rooms with air-conditioning, also a travel agency and hire car service. *31 rooms, Pahonyothin Road, Tel. 053/71 13 39, Fax 71 39 63, Category 3*

ENTERTAINMENT

Limited to one or two bars and restaurants in the vicinity of the clock tower in *Thrapkaset Plaza, Jet Yot Road.*

INFORMATION

Tourism Authority of Thailand (TAT)

Open daily 8.30 am–4.30 pm, Sing-haklai Road, Tel. 053/71 74 33, Fax 71 74 34

SURROUNDING AREA

Mae Salong   (99/D 1)

Following Mao's communist revolution in China in 1949, this village (also called *Santi Khiri*), situated on the flank of the 1,800 m-high *Doi Mae Salong*, 50 km north-west of Chiang Rai, became a refuge for Kuomintang soldiers who fled across Burma into Thailand. Two generations later, the Kuomintang as they are still known, cultivate tea, coffee and vegetables. Profitably too judging from some of their houses near the frontier.

Many Chinese wares are sold on the market, which also attracts folk from the hill tribe villages. The town's history is documented in a little museum in the rather dilapidated *Mae Salong Resort.* The wooden bungalows of the *Khumnaipol Resort (24 rooms, Tel. 053/76 50 01, Fax 76 50 04, Category 3)* offer pleasant accommodation with a view of the town.

Thaton (99/D 1)

⭐ Situated on the Kok River 80 km west of Chiang Rai, Thaton is the starting point for rafting trips down river to the provincial capital. Two nights are spent on the way (aboard the raft, in cabins ashore or in sleeping bags round a camp fire). Although the hillsides along the river have been almost completely cleared of trees, this tour is one of the most delightful and certainly one of the most relaxing of any you will find here in the north. Stops are made at hill villages en route. N.B. The covered bamboo rafts are very small for a full complement of five (plus two crew). It is much better all round if the number of passengers is limited to four, who can then expect to pay between about Bahts 1,500 and 2,000 each.

The night before setting off down river can be spent in one of several extremely simple guest houses, or the considerably more comfortable *Mae Kok River Lodge (Tel. 053/21 53 66, Category 3)* located by the river. For Bahts 180 anyone in a hurry can opt for one of the noisy speedboats which make the journey between Thaton and Chiang Rai in four to five (thoroughly exhausting) hours.

MAE HONG SON

(98/B 3) ⭐ The smallest Thai provincial capital (Pop. 11,000) is also one of the quietest. Situated near the Myanmar border and encircled by mountains, it was at one time dubbed "Siberia" on account of its remoteness. The surrounding country is ideal for exploring off the beaten tourist track.

The shortest route from Chiang Mai winds its way for 245 km through the mountains via *Pai*. You can also fly to Mae Hong Son for only Bahts 350 (30 minutes; Thailand's cheapest inland flight).

SIGHTS

Chong Kham Lake

A small lake with a park right in the town centre, particularly enchanting in the early morning when mist still swirls about and the water lilies begin to unfurl. At the water's edge stand a pair of temples *Wat Chong Klang* and *Wat Chong Kham*, filigree-like, in appearance. There can be few more idyllic sights.

Doi Kong Mu

〰️ This 424 m-high hill on the edge of the town is crowned by the snow-white chedi of *Wat Phra That Doi Kong Mu*. It affords a lovely view of the town, the valley and the mountains.

RESTAURANTS

There are food stands in *Khunlumpraphat Road* as well as several little restaurants by the lake.

Bai Fern Restaurant

Mae Hong Son's gourmet temple, or as close to it as it gets. *Khunlumpraphat Road, Tel. 053/61 13 74, Category 3*

HOTELS

Holiday Inn

With a large pool and excellent

restaurant. *114 rooms, Khun-lumpraphat Road (1 km from the centre), Tel 053/61 22 12, Fax 61 15 24, Category 1–2*

Piya Guest House

⚘ Simple rooms with air-conditioning or fan, in the best lakeside location. *14 rooms, Khunlumpraphat Road, Tel. 053/61 12 60, Fax 61 23 08, Category 3* (there are other simple guest houses around the lake)

Rim Nam Klang Doi Resort

Pretty wooden bungalows in a neat garden right beside the Pai River. A place to relax. *39 rooms, Ban Huai Dua (8 km out of town), Tel. 053/61 21 42, Fax 61 10 86, Category 3*

INFORMATION

Tourist Police

The *Tourist Police* represent the Tourism Authority in this particular area. *Singhanat Bamrung Road, Tel. 053/61 18 12*

SURROUNDING AREA

Tour operators and local guest houses offer interesting excursions and trekking as well as rafting on the Pai River.

Villages of the Long-Neck Women   (98/A 3)

One of the less palatable tourist attractions. A number of so-called *Long Necks*, women of the Padaung tribe, a sub-group of the Karen, whose necks appear elongated through the wearing of brass rings, have been brought over from Myanmar and settled in two villages set up for the purpose. One is in the jungle, the other on the Pai River a short distance from the frontier. Even the Padaung themselves speak privately of "human zoos". You pay Bahts 300 to enter the villages, and an extra Bahts 100 if you have a video camera.

To the frontier

A ⚏ track leads through wild and lonely mountain scenery to the Kuomintang village of *Mae Aw* (**98/A 2**). Since there are repeated skirmishes on the other side of the border between Burmese government forces and the hill tribes fighting for independence, the trip should only be undertaken with a guide who knows the area well.

Caves   (98/B 2)

A number of caves, many scarcely investigated, lie to the north-west of Mae Hong Son. *Tham Nam Lang* is thought to be one of the largest cave systems in the world. From the village of *Soppong* you can visit *Tham Lot*, a stalactitic cave. Not far away an Australian, John Spiess, has built ⚘ *Cave Lodge.* With its bamboo cabins the lodge makes a good base from which to explore the area.

MAE SAI

(**99/E 1**) Thailand's most northerly town (Pop. 5,000) lies 62 km from Chiang Rai. A bridge crosses the narrow Mae Sai River to *Tachilek* in Myanmar. Foreigners are allowed over during the day, paying US$ 5 on the Burmese side.

SHOPPING

Chinese wares, contraband cigarettes and an assortment of handicrafts can be purchased on the market in ★ Tachilek. Beware of "bargain" gemstones, they are just coloured glass. You can also buy craftwork in Mae Sai.

Mae Sai Guest House
Simple bungalows, prettily situated on a grassy site by the river, 1 km west of the bridge. *15 rooms, Tel. 053/73 20 21, Category 3*

Between it and the bridge are a number of cheap guest houses, including the extraordinary ★ *Mae Sai Plaza (Tel. 053/73 22 30, Category 3)*, a string of cabins clinging to the hillside.

Wang Thong Hotel
This hotel (with pool), located a short distance east of the bridge, is incomparably the best Mae Sai has to offer. *148 rooms, Phaho-nyothin Road, Tel. 053/73 38 89-95, Fax 73 33 99, Category 2–3*

Golden Triangle   (99/E 1)
Half an hour's journey away by road is the notorious *Golden Triangle*, where you arrive to find the Mekong almost obscured by souvenir stalls. The small but interesting *Opium Museum (entrance Bahts 20)* explains how the drug is produced and traditionally smoked. From a *viewpoint* above a small monastery you can see Thailand, Laos and Myanmar, the three countries which meet here and make up the "triangle".

On the Thai side, lightning fast speedboats with noisy engines can be hired for river trips. But beware! Under no circumstances set foot ashore on either Laotian or Burmese territory.

Famous but no longer infamous: the Golden Triangle on the Mekong

Where tradition remains strong

In the land of the rice farmers – hot on the trail of dinosaurs and ancient cultures

The high plateau of the north-east, like the central plain north of Bangkok, is a land of rice farmers. But here in the Isan, an area of low rainfall, the ground is barren and the harvests often small. In summer, when the oppressive heat bears down like a curse on the dusty soil, many a grain of rice shrivels on the stalk. The north-east is the poorhouse of the country, unable to provide for all its inhabitants. Many have migrated to Bangkok and other parts of Thailand blessed with more favoured conditions and economies.

KHON KAEN

(104/B 2) This university town of 180,000 people, in the very heart of the Isan, 450 km from Bangkok, is the region's unofficial capital. Few tourists stop off at Khon Kaen. Apart from its extremely well endowed National Museum, the town itself has no attractions to speak of.

In many villages in the Isan, rice is still threshed by hand

SIGHTS

Bung Kaen Nakhon

The lake on the south-eastern edge of the city centre is a favourite recreation spot for the locals. The pyramid-shaped, red, white and gold-bedecked *Wat Muang Gao* boasts exquisite carvings on the doors and windows.

MUSEUM

National Museum

The museum has a large collection of archaeological finds of great interest, including stone and bronze axes from *Ban Chiang*, boundary stones dating from the 9th and 10th centuries decorated with reliefs of Buddha, a charming bronze Buddha of the Sukhothai period, markedly feminine in face, and an 11th century figure of Shiva. There is also a reconstruction of a traditional farmhouse. *Wed–Sun 9 am–4 pm, entrance Bahts 30, Langsunratchakan Road*

RESTAURANTS

In the ☻ night bazaar, for just a few Bahts, you can eat your fill of traditional Isan cooking.
For a pleasant sit-down meal

try the open restaurants in the *Night Garden Plaza,* near the *Kosa Hotel.* Much the best places to eat, though, offering food of a quality not lightly to be forgone, are the restaurants in the *Hotel Sofitel.*

HOTELS

Hotel Sofitel Raja Orchid

It is almost worth travelling to the Isan simply for the pleasure of staying at one of the region's five-star hotels. Even a so-called *junior suite* will only cost you about Bahts 2,650. In Bangkok it would be three or four times the price.

The hotel's three restaurants (Thai, Chinese, Vietnamese) are outstanding and by no means outrageously expensive. *293 rooms, Prachasumran Road, Tel. 043/32 21 55, Fax 32 21 50, www.Sofitel.com, Category L–1*

Kosa Hotel

Why stint yourself when for just a few Bahts more you can enjoy the extra comfort and opulence of a deluxe room? You won't find better value for money anywhere. The only drawback is the lack of a pool. And even then, hotel guests are able to use the pool in the neighbouring shopping centre. *187 rooms, Srichan Road, Tel. 043/32 03 20, Fax 22 50 13, Category 2–3*

ENTERTAINMENT

In addition to being the best hotel, the Sofitel Raja Orchid is also the centre of the town's night-life. In the *Underground Entertainment Complex* you find not only the most modern discotheque in the region but the largest karaoke studio as well, not forgetting food stands serving many Asiatic specialities.

INFORMATION

Tourism Authority of Thailand (TAT)

Information office open daily 8.30

MARCO POLO SELECTION: THE NORTH-EAST

1 Nong Khai
A delightful small town on the Mekong River, and an extraordinary sculpture park (page 69)

2 Phimai
An ancient banyan tree and the loveliest Khmer temple in Thailand (page 68)

3 Ban Chiang
Exploring the remains of an advanced Bronze Age culture (page 71)

4 The silk-weavers' village
Where you can watch as shimmering Thai silk is woven (page 68)

5 Jumbo festival
Parade of skills at the annual elephant round-up in Surin (page 70)

6 Dinosaur Park
In the province of Khon Kaen, gigantic dinosaurs point the way to fossil excavation sites (page 67)

Cobra: star of the show in the village of Khoksanga

am–4.30 pm, Prachasamosorn Road, Tel. 043/24 44 98-9, Fax 24 44 97

SURROUNDING AREA

Attempting to fully explore this area relying solely on public transport can be a complicated business. However cars can be hired, with or without a driver, through *Kaen Koon Travel (Ammart Road, Tel. 043/23 94 58)*. The *Sofitel Raja Orchid* also arranges tours.

Phu Wiang National Park   (104/B 1)
⭐ The park advertises itself as "Dinosaurland". The gigantic saurian sculptures are of recent date, but the fossilized relics of these prehistoric creatures are 120 to 140 million years old. There are excavation sites and fossil finds to be seen and, in the little visitors' centre, informative displays to study. *80 km north-west of Khon Kaen*

Ubolrat Dam and Cobra Village
⚙ The 800 m-long Ubolrat Dam (**104/A–B 1–2**) lies some 50 km north-west of Khon Kaen. Extending over an area of 410 sq km, the reservoir is a popular place for excursions and leisure activities, with boat trips and its own golf course. A trip there can be combined with a visit to the village of *Ban Khoksanga* (**104/B 1**), where the *King Cobra Conservation Project* keeps cobras and other snakes in enclosures. Men from the village put on a show of wrestling with the snakes. If you go during the week you are likely to be the only visitors, so be sure to ask how much the show will cost beforehand.

NAKHON RATCHASIMA

(**104/A 4**) Commonly known as *Korat*, Nakhon Ratchasima (Pop. 200,000), capital of its province, is the largest city in the region and gateway to the north-east. It is also the most important industrial centre and a major junction upon which routes from all directions converge. Most of the sights of interest are located in the countryside around. Rail, bus and plane connections to Bangkok are good.

SIGHTS

Thao Suranari Monument
Dedicated to Thao Suranari, revered as a national heroine for her courage in defending the city against Laotian invaders in 1826. *Ratchadamnoen Road*

MUSEUM

Maha Wirawong National Museum
The museum boasts a collection containing many figures of Buddha, ceramics, carvings and examples of Khmer art. *Open Wed–Sun 9 am–4 pm, entrance Bahts 10, Ratchadamnoen Road, in the grounds of Wat Suthachinda*

RESTAURANTS

☼ During the day food stands are open on the market opposite the Thao Suranari Monument, in the evening at the *night bazaar, Mahattai Road/corner of Manat Road*

Pokaphan
Typical Isan food, including some of the more distinctive dishes, for example fish-stomach soup. *Asdang Road, Tel. 044/24 25 68, Category 3*

HOTELS

Chomsurang
Comfortable rooms at favourable prices; pool; central. *167 rooms, Mahattai Road, Tel. 044/25 70 88-9, Fax 25 28 97, Category 2–3*

Royal Princess
The best hotel in the city centre. With a very good Chinese restaurant. *188 rooms, Suranari Road, Tel. 044/25 66 29, Fax 25 66 01, Category 1*

INFORMATION

Tourism Authority of Thailand (TAT)
N.B. Because in the Isan relatively few people speak English, it is important to have maps (obtainable here) with your destination in Thai. *Open daily 8.30 am–4.30 pm, Mittraphap Road (bypass on the edge of town, near the Hotel Sima Thani), Tel. 044/21 36 66, Fax 21 36 67*

SURROUNDING AREA

Silk-weavers' village (104/A 5)
★ Here you can follow the process of silk manufacture and watch silk fabrics being woven by hand as well as on modern looms. In the village of *Pak Thong Chai. 32 km south, shuttle bus service*

Potters' village (104/A 4–5)
In *Dan Kwian* ceramic wares are manufactured in the traditional manner – and sold at almost unbelievably low prices. *15 km south, regular local buses*

Phimai (104/A 4)
★ In the middle of the pleasant little town of *Phimai, (60 km northeast, plenty of buses)* is the largest Khmer temple complex outside Cambodia. The *Phimai Historical Park (open daily 7.30 am–6 pm, entrance Bahts 20)* comprises a series of imposing sandstone buildings grouped around a central 28 m-high prang. Also not to be missed is

the *Phimai National Museum (Open Wed–Sun 8 am–4.30 pm, entrance Bahts 10)* which has a collection of works of art and archaeological finds from the Isan. On the banks of the *Mun River, (2 km east of the town)*, nature has produced its own work of art – a huge, centuries-old banyan tree known as *Sai Ngam*.

Accommodation can be found at the extremely simple but centrally situated ☀ *Old Phimai Guest House (8 rooms, Chomsudasadet Road, Tel. 044/47 19 18, Category 3)* or in the air-conditioned rooms of the *Phimai Inn (Tel. 044/47 11 75, Category 3, about 1.5 km from the town on By-Pass Road)*. Phimai's most popular restaurant is the *Bai-Teiy (Chomsudasadet Road, Category 3)*, where you can enjoy good, reasonably priced Thai food.

Phrasat Phanom Rung   (104/B 4)

◁◁▷ This temple complex, *100 km east of Korat* in the province of Buri Ram, is among the greatest masterpieces of Khmer architecture in Thailand. Built in the 12th century on an extinct volcano, reaching it by public transport is a laborious business. Cars with drivers can be hired in Korat from, e.g. the *Korat Business Co. (Buarong Road, Tel. 044/25 86 31-2)*.

NONG KHAI

(100/C 5) ★ This small provincial capital of 25,000 inhabitants offers restful, relaxing days by the Mekong River. The economic boom which many people hoped for when the bridge across the Mekong to Laos was built, has never materialized. Only very few cars drive over the 1.2 km *Thai-Lao Friendship Bridge* to the Laotian capital Vientiane, 22 km away.

SIGHTS

Wat Khaek's bizarre sculpture garden provides a spectacle that is utterly unique – gigantic (concrete) figures of Buddha, Hindu gods, demons clutching decapitated heads, seven-headed cobras, ele-

Picnic on the bank of the Mekong in Nong Khai

69

phants, and many more, measured against which even the tallest visitor is dwarfed. *3 km east*

RESTAURANTS

There are lots of small restaurants catering for Western travellers, e.g. *Nobbi's (Mecchai Road, Tel. 042/46 05 83, Category 3)* where, in addition to purveying his homemade sausage and pineapple juice, the proprietor arranges tours. ☆ The *Rueae Pae Haisoke, (Category 3)* is a floating restaurant near *Wat Haisoke*; every evening at 5.30 pm a boat trip sets off for a one-hour cruise with dinner on the Mekong. *Le Bistro, (Rimkong Road, Tel. 042/41 22 29, Category 3)*, serves Thai and French dishes enjoyed looking out over the river. There are also Thai restaurants by *Sadet Market* (on the pier). When the water in the Mekong is low, food stands set up on the sand banks near the bridge.

SHOPPING

A wide range of goods from Laos and China are among those on sale in the *Sadet Market*.

Village Weaver Handicrafts
This self-help project has its own shop offering a large selection of handwoven fabrics and clothes. You can also watch the women who produce them at work. *Prachak Road, Tel. 042/41 12 36*

HOTELS

Mekong Royal Nongkai
Well furnished rooms, large pool; right by the Mekong, 500 m upstream of the bridge. *197 rooms, Jommanee Beach, Tel.*

042/42 00 24, Fax 42 12 80, Category 2

Mut Mee Guest House
☀ Extremely simple bungalows, some without showers of their own, but right on the embankment by the river. Good rustic-style restaurant in the garden. A favourite with travellers, but embassy staff from Vientiane enjoy time off here too. Run by an Englishman, Julian, and his wife Pao, who also lay on courses in yoga, hire out bicycles and arrange tours. *26 rooms, Kaaeworawat Road, Fax 042/46 07 17, e-mail wasambe@loxinfo.co.th, Category 3.* There are several other simple guest houses in the vicinity.

INFORMATION

Tourism Authority of Thailand (TAT)
Information office open daily 8.30 am–4.30 pm, Mitrapap Thai-Lao Road, Tel./Fax 042/46 78 44

SURROUNDING AREA

Surin   (104/C 4–5)
Every year in November this town of 40,000 people, capital of Surin province, is inundated with tourists for the annual ☀ *elephant round-up* on the third weekend of the month. As many as 200 elephants show off the tricks taught them by members of the Suay tribe. Bangkok travel agencies arrange special trips by train or bus. In the "elephant village" of Ta Klang, 60 km north of Surin, there is a little museum dedicated to the animals, where you can also see how they are trained. These displays usually take place at weekends (enquire at your hotel for the latest information).

Comfortable accommodation is found at the *Petchkasem Hotel (162 rooms, Chitbamrung Road, Tel. 044/51 12 74, Fax 51 10 41, Category 2-3)*; pool, restaurant, folk music. The ☆ *Pirom Guest House (8 rooms, Krungsinai Road, Tel 044/51 51 40, Category 3)* is spartan, but Pirom knows the area well and organizes tours. Ron Barber at the *Country Roads restaurant (Sirirat Road, Tel. 044/51 57 21, Category 3)* also provides hand-outs. *Surin is situated 200 km east of Korat and is easily reached by bus or train*

UDON THANI

(100/C 6) This commercial centre (Pop. 100,000) lies on the railway between Khon Kaen and Nong Khai. Although Udon Thani province boasts the most significant archaeological site in Thailand (the Bronze Age site at *Ban Chiang*), the town itself is not a tourist destination. Access is by plane, train or bus.

SIGHTS

Udon Sunshine Orchid Garden
Not only does Mr Pradit breed orchids here, he has also extracted perfume from them – a unique achievement in Thailand. But what really draws people to his Sunshine Orchid Garden are Mr Pradit's "dancing plants". When sung to in a gentle voice, these hybrids, bred from Thai and Chinese foliage plants, move their leaves. *Nongsamrong Road, Tel. 042/24 24 75, entrance Bahts 50 (proceeds to the AIDS charity)*

HOTELS

Charoensri Grand Royal Hotel
The best in Udon Thani, situated directly opposite the shopping centre; pool and fitness centre. Very good value for money. *255 rooms, Prachak Road, Tel. 042/34 35 55, Fax 34 35 50, Category 2*

Roland's Guest House
Well cared for urban resort hotel, with pool, sauna and fitness centre. All rooms have air-conditioning, television and minibar. Car and motorcycle hire service. *18 rooms, Srichomchuen Road, Tel. 042/24 61 59 and 01/9 54 56 97, Fax 24 67 16, Category 3*

INFORMATION

Tourism Authority of Thailand (TAT)
Information office open daily 8.30 am–4.30 pm, Mukmontri Road, Tel. 042/32 54 06-7, Fax 32 54 08

Kannika Tour
Kannika, speaks good English. She arranges tours (e.g. to Laos), and hires out bicycles. *Srisatha Road, Tel. 042/24 13 78, Fax 24 04 43*

SURROUNDING AREA

Ban Chiang **(101/D 6)**
★ 3,500 years ago, a highly sophisticated farming community lived on the site of this small village 56 km east of Udon. Finds unearthed here, pottery, bronze tools, skeletons, form the basis of the small but impressive *National Museum* established with the aid of American experts. In the courtyard of *Wat Phi Si Nai* the site of one of the digs is preserved and open to the public. Modern-day Ban Chiang potters sell very authentic-looking wares in front of the museum. *Wed–Sun 9 am–4.30 pm, entrance Bahts 30*

A holiday paradise both above and below the water

Heavenly beaches, uninhabited islands and tree houses in the jungle

It's no exaggeration to say that the south of Thailand is exactly as you might imagine a holiday paradise to be – so beautiful scenically as to make even the most seasoned traveller catch their breath in delight, and varied enough to satisfy the most divergent of interests. Whether you seek peace and quiet or all action and excitement (or both), you'll find yourself utterly spoilt for choice. On the beaches, in particular those on the islands in the Gulf of Siam and off the shores of the Andaman Sea, the dreams of holidaymakers from all over the world are realised.

Nature has been kind to the inhabitants of southern Thailand. Even before the arrival of the tourists with their foreign currencies, these lucky folk lacked for nothing. The fish in the sea, the fertile soil, and buried treasures such as tin, ensured a relatively carefree existence – and,

The salt water pool at the Tonsai Bay resort on Ko Samui

for many who lived here, even riches. Of course tourism has become an increasingly important factor in the economy of the region, but only on two islands, Phuket and Samui, is it the lynchpin on which the local economy overridingly depends. And even then, there are some for whom the traditional fabric of life continues much as before.

This chapter lists, in alphabetical order, firstly destinations on and in the Gulf of Siam (east coast), secondly those on and in the Andaman Sea (west coast).

HUA HIN

(**106/B 3**) In the days when Thailand was still known as Siam, royalty would come here to bathe at the oldest resort in the country. Nowadays most people you see on the miles of beaches are weekend visitors from Bangkok, 240 kilometres away. Though there are apartment blocks strung all along the seafront, the town of 60,000 inhabitants contrives to remain an oasis of tranquility, exactly as the travel brochures describe it. Weathered wooden pile dwellings still stand on the beach, and no excursion craft vie with the fishing boats for moorings. A good proportion of the tourists who come here from abroad have already left nightlong disco dancing behind them, preferring the pleasures of a resort which sparkles with the charm of a delightful old lady. And that is a quality which it will take far more than a few newly built hotels to alter.

SIGHTS

Khao Takiab Hill

This craggy hill can be seen rising at the southern end of the beach. The view from the *temple* is absolutely superb. The monkeys there are very partial to bananas.

RESTAURANTS

There are many restaurants serving international cuisine, as well as many fish restaurants, along *Naradamri Road*, which runs parallel to the beach. The mussel omelettes and noodle soup with duck in the ✪ night bazaar are delicious.

HOTELS

A host of little guest houses and small hotels are to be found in the tourist district between the seafront and the town centre.

Hotel Sofitel Central

Built in the nineteen twenties in the Victorian style, this hotel combines luxury with a big dollop of nostalgia. Wonderfully beautiful park with animal topi-

ary. Located right by the beach. *218 rooms, Tel. 032/51 20 21-35, Fax 51 10 14, Category 1*

Jed Pee Nong

Functional air-conditioned rooms, small pool, 200 metres from the beach. *50 rooms, Tel. 032/51 23 81, Fax 53 20 63, Category 2–3*

INFORMATION

Tourist Information Center

Located in the government offices.
Open daily 8.30 am–4.30 pm, Phetkasem Road, Tel. 032/51 10 47

SURROUNDING AREA

Travel agents offer a large number of tours to places as yet barely exploited by the tourist industry, for example to the *Khao Sam Roi Yot National Park* where there are massive limestone cliffs both on land and under the water, or into the jungle to the *Palua U Falls* near the border with Myanmar. On the trip to the neighbouring province of Petchaburi to the north, you take the cable car up *Khao Wang*, on the top of which is perched King Mongkut's summer palace. A little further north, in *Ratchaburi* (**106/B 1**), you can watch as millions of bats emerge from the *Khan Khao* cave at sunset, looking for all the world like an enormous flying carpet.

KO SAMUI

(**109/E 3**) As the plane makes its approach to the runway of the primitive airport, which comprises little more than a thatched roof on stilts, Thailand's third

MARCO POLO SELECTION: THE SOUTH

1 Ko Phi Phi
Thailand's loveliest island, with spectacular rock formations and creamy-white beaches (page 83)

2 Phang Nga
Bay of limestone cliffs, sugarloaves and stacks and a pile village in the sea (page 83)

3 Ko Lanta
Leaving civilisiation behind on a dreamy island away from the tourist throng (page 78)

4 Khao Sok National Park
Where you go down into the jungle and up into the tree houses (page 83)

5 A canopied bed high above the sea
The Tonsai Bay resort on the island of Ko Samui: exorbitantly expensive but breathtakingly beautiful (page 77)

6 Party time
The disco scene on Ko Samui – turning up the heat dancing the night away (page 77)

largest island looks like a vast coconut plantation crowned by hill jungle. So even before you arrive you are likely to have fallen in love with this holiday paradise on the Gulf of Siam. There are no traffic jams here to send your blood pressure rocketing; legs are the only thing you need to thoroughly familiarise yourself with this island's "metropolis". Everywhere is green, and beaches and bays follow one upon another like a string of beads. It is no wonder that, prior to the airport being constructed in 1988, Ko Samui had long been a favourite among rucksack travellers. Since then, as the more affluent type of tourist has "discovered" this little tropical gem, most of the bamboo cabins have had to make way for more comfortable resorts. But the authorities on Ko Samui are very mindful of the need to avoid the architec-tural eyesores which so disfigure Phuket. Although there are no sights to speak of on Ko Samui, boredom doesn't have a chance to set in; this isle of coconut palms is not only a wonderful place to bathe but also overflow-ing with party spirit.

BEACHES

Most of the island's resorts and the best facilities are to be found on the beaches of *Chaweng* (the nicest of all) and *Lamai* on the east coast. There, bays such as *Thong Sai, Choeng Mon, Chaweng Noi, Coral Cove* and *Na Khai* are little oases of tranquility. A simi-lar calm reigns over *Mae Nam, Bo Phut* and *Big Buddha* beaches on the north coast. The south and west coasts of the island have hardly been developed as yet. Here the beaches are much less attractive and the water shallow, good only for swimming.

SIGHTS

The island, which has an area of only 247 sq km, can be explored comfortably in a day via its 51 kilometre circumference road. In the course of the tour you can visit the *Monkey Theatre* with its monkey and elephant show *(10.30 am, and 2 and 4 pm, entrance Bahts 150)* and a *butterfly farm (Bahts 120)*, as well as the new *aquarium (Bahts 250)* opened in 1999. Also well worth while are detours to the island's principal landmark, the 15 metre-high ◁▷ *Big Buddha*, and the *Hin Lad* and *Namuang* waterfalls. In the out-of-the-way fishing village of ◉ *Hua Thanon* in the south-east of the island you can see boats decorated with carvings and colourfully painted. From time to time (bloodless) buffalo fights are staged in makeshift arenas, water-buffaloes being encouraged to test their strength while the locals wager enthusiastically on the outcome. Make enquiries at your hotel reception about times and places.

RESTAURANTS

It's only at Chaweng Beach and Lamai Beach that you find any real choice of restaurants. Otherwise you are dependent on whichever resort you are staying at for (more or less imaginative) meals. The Thai food on the food stands e.g. in the *Lamai Food Center*, or in the simpler type of restaurant, is often better (and cheaper) than in those catering expressly for tourists. By far the best places to dine are the restaurants in the high-class resorts, for example the *Santiburi Dusit* resort

(Mae Nam), *Thongsai Bay* (Thong Sai) and *Imperial Samui* (Chaweng Noi).

Drop Inn

Italian cooking in an unusual wooden building, lit by thousands of fairy lights in the evening. *Open daily 5 pm–midnight, Chaweng Beach, Tel. 077/23 03 61, Category 3)*

Sala Thai

One of the better Thai restaurants apart from the hotels (but the Western dishes are best ignored). *Open daily 4–11.30 pm, Lamai Beach, Tel. 077/23 31 80, Category 3)*

Wild Orchid

Seafood and real Thai cuisine, spiced to suit Western palates. Pleasant atmosphere: half restaurant, half antique shop. *Open daily midday–11 pm, Chaweng Beach, Tel. 077/42 22 01, Category 2–3*

HOTELS

Laem Sai

Simple bungalows with air-conditioning or fan; very quiet position on a tongue of land dividing Mae Nam from Bo Phut. *25 rooms, Mae Nam Beach, Tel. 077/42 51 33, Category 2–3*

Laem Set Inn

Choice of bamboo huts or more luxurious wooden bungalows, some being converted from traditional houses. Wonderful setting, with pool; even the cheapest bungalows with air-conditioning cost Bahts 1,900. *27 rooms, Na Khai Bay (Hua Thanon), Tel. 077/42 43 93, Fax 42 43 94, www.laemset.com, Category L–2*

Ko Samui: blue water, green palms, white sand

Montien House

Pleasant tidy site amidst a profusion of greenery; neat bungalows with or without air-conditioning, television. *48 rooms, Chaweng Beach, Tel. 077/42 21 69, Fax 42 21 45, e-mail montien@samart.co.th., Category 2–3*

Royal Blue Lagoon

Romantic little complex with comfortable air-conditioned bungalows. Small pool. *17 rooms, Lamai Beach, Tel. 077/23 11 80-1, Fax 42 41 95, Category 2*

The Spa

Extremely basic bungalows, a place for the health food-conscious (also meditation, massage, sauna, vegetarian meals, yoga). *18 rooms, Lamai Beach, Tel. 077/ 23 08 55, www.surat.loxinfo.co.th/ ~thespa, Category 3*

The Tonsai Bay

★ ☆ Absolutely top class resort. Natural sea water pool complete with sand and rocks. The bungalows are spread out over the slopes around the little bay. Best of all are the 160 sq metre suites, with two baths and a canopied bed on the terrace high above the sea. *72 rooms, Ban Plailem, Bophut, Tel. 077/42 50 15-28, Fax 42 54 62, e-mail tongsai@loxinfo.co.th, Category L*

SPORTS & LEISURE

There are facilities for every kind of watersport, with most choice at Chaweng Beach and Lamai Beach. There is also a go-cart track, a mini-golf course and a shooting range. Several tour operators organize elephant trekking.

ENTERTAINMENT

★ On Ko Samui there's partying every night, right through to early morning. The island's night-life is centred on the pubs and discotheques, some of which are huge. When ★ *The Doors Pub* at Chaweng proclaims "If you find it too loud, you're too old!" it speaks for all of them. Other in-places at Chaweng are the vast, wooden ★ *Reggae Pub*, where Bob Marley used to live it up, and ★ *The Club* which presents a broad mix of music. At the ★ *Green Mango* and in particular at the ⚲ *Santa Fe* (a techno temple in the style of an Aztec citadel), things only really get going at 2 or 3 am when the other discos close. At Lamai Beach you can mingle with a mainly Thai crowd at the ☯ *Mix Pub* (which stages drag shows and Thai boxing as well) or sample the entertainment at the ⚲ *Bauhaus* – including videos projected on huge screens – before moving on to dance the rest of the night away in the ⚲ *Rock Pub*.

INFORMATION

Tourism Authority of Thailand (TAT)
Open daily 8.30 am–4 pm, Nathon, Nathon Road (to the right of the pier, by the post office), Tel. 077/42 14 36

Internet
www.sawadee.com,
www.samuiwelcome.com

SURROUNDING AREA

Ang Thong National Park (109/E 3)
The archipelago of 40 uninhabited islands between Ko Samui and the mainland is good for snorkelling; all the travel agents arrange day trips. By far the most interesting way to explore this marine park though is by kayak.

Ko Phangan   (109/E 3)
⚲ Ko Samui's smaller sister (191 sq km) may only be half an hour away by ferry but the two islands are worlds apart. Ko Phangan is hill jungle set in the sea, inhabited by just a few thousand fishermen and coconut growers. It is the island with the craziest mix of tourists in the whole of Thailand, the beach bungalows, most of

which are pretty spartan, being occupied by ageing hippies, introverted diarists, back-to-nature enthusiasts, meditators, escapees from civilization and perfectly normal holidaymakers. The high point of island life is the monthly *full moon party* on *Rin Beach*, which attracts both tourists and a contingent of police from Ko Samui. When the music on the beach becomes loud enough to be heard in Bangkok, anyone who hasn't got at least one earring or a tattoo to show, somehow just doesn't seem to fit in.

By far the best island resort is the *Panviman (50 rooms, Tel./Fax 077/37 70 48, Category 2)* on the superb isolated beach at Tong Nai Pan in the north-east of the island. A small tourist village and most of the rest of the accommodation is located at the infamous Rin Beach. Pick of the bunch is the *Orchid Resort (Category 3)*, a perfectly acceptable place to stay.

Ko Tao   (109/E 2)
Around this little island 60 kilometres north of Ko Samui lie the best diving grounds in the Gulf of Siam, where even whale sharks can be spotted from time to time. Accommodation is available in many simple resorts, e.g. *Ko Ta Cottage (Tel. 01/725 07 51, Category 3)*. There are ferries to and from Ko Samui and Ko Phangan.

KO LANTA

(110/A 3) ⭐ Ko Lanta is still relatively new ground for tourists despite being easily accessible by ferry from Ko Phi Phi and Krabi. Along the 20 km of the island's west coast there are a number of beaches with simple resorts.

Traffic on the track-road is limited to a few pick-up trucks. *Ban Saladan*, where the ferry boats tie up, is just a string of weather-darkened houses along a single village street.

RESTAURANTS

The only real choice of restaurants is on the main *Klong Dao Beach* where *Hans* makes tasty *Kässpätzle* (a kind of noodles with cheese), and on Sundays *Danny's* lays on a *Festival of Thai Food*. At the other beaches you have to rely on the resort kitchens. Robert, of the *Saladan Swiss Bakery* at *Ban Saladan* pier, serves fresh bread with ham and real coffee.

HOTELS

Lanta Villa
Simple, functional bungalows, some with air-conditioning. Good restaurant (but it's best to resist the Western-style food). *40 rooms, Klong Dao Beach, Tel./Fax 075/62 06 29, Category 3*

Relax Bay Tropicana
Simple wooden bungalows (fan, shower) on the steep hillside above a small bay; dive centre. *48 rooms, Phra Ae Beach, Tel. 01/722 00 89, 075/62 06 18, Category 3*

SPORTS & LEISURE

The resorts organise snorkelling trips to the off-shore islets. Dive centres such as the German-run *Ko Lanta Diving* and *Atlantis Diving* in Ban Saladan take you out to the underwater reefs at *Hin Muang* where whale sharks and rays are a common sight.

KRABI

(108/C 6) From a scenic point of view the coastline of this mainland province situated to the south of Phuket is surely the most beautiful of any in Thailand. The best beaches, at Phra Nang and Railay, are accessible only by boat (from the main Ao Nang Beach, a trip of approximately 10 minutes), being cut off on the shore side by limestone cliffs. Since these two beaches are only a few hundred metres long, they tend to get rather overcrowded in high season.

SIGHTS

Ko Poda
A tiny rocky island with a snow-white beach, about 20 minutes by boat from Ao Nang Beach. A good spot for snorkelling. The 18 *Poda bungalows (Category 3)* provide the only accommodation; bookings through *Krabi Resort (Ao Nang Beach, Tel. 075/63 70 30-5, Fax 63 70 51-2, Category 2–3)*

Phra Nang Cave and Princess Lagoon
In the cave at Phra Nang Beach there is a shrine with votive offerings in the form of gigantic wooden phalluses – said to ensure the blessing of children and other forms of good fortune. After an arduous climb of some 150 metres, you can peer down into a little lagoon which at high tide fills with sea water via a tunnel in the rock.

Temple of the Tiger Cave
Wat Tam Sua is a cliff monastery about 6 km from Krabi town. An extremely steep

Mountain in the sea: Krabi's beaches are spectacular

staircase of 1,272 steps leads up a hill, the caves in which form part of the monastery. The view justifies every drop of perspiration.

RESTAURANTS

The best choice of restaurants is at Ao Nang Beach, to which buses run from the provincial capital Krabi. There are seafood restaurants at *Soi Sunset*, right along at the narrow north end of the beach. The *Last Café* occupies an idyllic position at the opposite, southern end.

HOTELS

Especially at Phra Nang and Railay there is a lot of simpler-style accommodation attractive mainly to younger people.

Dusit Rayavadee Resort
This is one of the best and most exclusive beach resorts in the country, with particularly elegant circular bungalows set in a palm grove beneath high cliffs where monkeys clamber. For about Bahts 25,000 per night you can occupy a villa with a pool and jacuzzi. *100 rooms, Phra Nang Beach, Tel. 075/62 07 40-3, Fax 62 06 30, www.dusit.com, Category L*

Peace Laguna Resort
Functional bungalows (air-conditioning or fan) by a lagoon five minutes away from the beach. *38 rooms, Ao Nang Beach, Tel. 075/63 73 45-6, Fax 63 73 47, Category 2–3*

Sand Sea Bungalow
Simple but solidly built bungalows with fan or air-conditioning. *60 rooms, Railay Beach, Tel. 01/722 01 14, Category 2–3*

SPORTS & LEISURE

Options include canoeing, diving and rock climbing – for which latter there is more than ample scope on the limestone cliffs abounding in the area (beginner's courses at Phra Nang Beach).

INFORMATION

Tourism Authority of Thailand (TAT)
Information office in Krabi town centre. *Open daily 8.30 am–4 pm, Utarakit Road, Tel. 075/61 27 40*

PHUKET

(108/B-C 6) Thailand's largest island has it all: first-class beaches by the dozen, varied scenery, a lively provincial capital and plenty of leisure activities. No wonder Phuket (Pop. 215,000) tops the list as South-East Asia's number one holiday isle. Of course there is considerably more to Phuket's emergence as a prime tourist destination than that; ease of access and excellent transport facilities (bridge to the mainland and an international airport) are further contributary factors.

BEACHES

The most attractive beaches are situated on the west coast and southern tip of the island, facing the open Andaman Sea. *Patong Beach*, lined with multi-storey hotels, is the beach with the most amenities, and therefore a bit of a circus. *Karon Beach* and *Kata Beach* are not quite as lively. The beaches at *Ao Sane, Bang Tao, Kamala, Karon Noi, Kata Noi, Nai Harn, Nai Yang, Naithon, Pansea and Surin* are in comparison relatively quiet.

SIGHTS

Phuket has a great many tourist attractions: these include a *snake farm (Patong Beach on the road to Karon, entrance Bahts 100, with show Bahts 200)*, a *zoo (near Phuket town, in the direction of Chalong, entrance with shows Bahts 400)*, a *crocodile farm (Phuket town, entrance Bahts 80, with show Bahts 250)* and a *butterfly farm (north edge of Phuket town, entrance Bahts 100)*. In the *Orchid Garden & Thai Village (edge of Phuket town, in the direction of the airport, entrance Bahts 250)*, there is folk music and dancing as well as orchids on display.

Marine Biological Research Centre

This research institute, also known as *Phuket Aquarium*, breeds turtles and keeps sharks and small fish in aquaria. *Open daily 10 am–4 pm, entrance Bahts 20, near Phuket town at Cape Phan Wa.*

Mangrove swamps

On the undeveloped *Mai Khao Beach* in the far north of the island you can follow a board walk through a section of mangrove forest in the *Sirirat National Park*.

Kao Phra Thaeo Park

The last remnants of virgin jungle in the north of the island. A trail leads to waterfalls. In the *Gibbon Rehabilitation Center*, gibbons which have been ill-treated as domestic pets are prepared for release back into the wild.

Cape Promthep

Bus loads of tourists flock to the southernmost tip of the island to photograph the setting sun. Better by far to make your way up to the *Promthep Cape Restaurant (Tel. 01/ 723 00 59, Category 3)* where you can sip a cocktail while simultaneously enjoying the fantastic view.

Phuket town

In the centre of the town (Pop. 60,000) you can still see plenty of old buildings in the Sino-Portuguese style, recalling the era of tin and rubber moguls.

Wat Chalong

At the time of the Thai and Chinese New Year festivals, large markets are held at the island's biggest monastery near the village of Chalong.

RESTAURANTS

Ka Jok Si

The very best in Thai cuisine dished up in an elderly townhouse oozing atmosphere. *Open daily except for Mon dinner, Phuket town, Takua Pa Road, Tel. 21 79 03, Category 2–3*

Luk Nut Restaurant

Garden restaurant with authentic Thai food served under an enormous rubber tree. On the road from Chalong to Rawai, past the *Island Resort turn-off. Open daily for* dinner, *Vises Road, Tel. 076/28 88 59, Category 3*

Sawasdee Thai Restaurant

They pride themselves here on their *Royal Thai Cuisine*, in which particular emphasis is placed on the appearance of the food. *Open daily from 5 pm, Phuket town, Mae Luan Road, Tel. 076/23 48 04, Category 2–3*

The Gallery Grill

Situated high above the sea between Kata and Kata Noi. Delicious combinations of Thai and Mediterranean cuisine. *Open daily for lunch and dinner, Patak Road, Tel. 076, 33 09 75, Category 1*

HOTELS

As far as accommodation goes, when it comes to value for money Phuket is undoubtedly the most expensive holiday destination in Thailand. And as long as the tourist boom continues, prices will inevitably be pushed up still further. Only very few resorts are situated right by the beach. It is absolutely essential to book in advance, especially around the New Year period.

Ao Sane Bungalows

In a semi-wild setting; few comforts but great if you like being close to nature (including snakes, frogs and wood rats). Small beach for snorkelling, but because of the sharp-edged coral and rocks it would be exceedingly dangerous to let young children bathe here. Periodic loud parties make this a place to be recommended for younger people only. *23 rooms, Ao Sane Beach, Tel./Fax 076/28 83 06, Category 3*

Banyan Tree Phuket

Elegant villas with gardens, some with their own pools. Health centre offering meditation, massage, sauna, yoga. By the beach. *78 rooms, Bang Tao Beach, Srisonthorn Road, Tel. 076/32 43 74, Fax 32 43 75, e-mail phuket@bany antree.com, Category L*

Peach Hill Hotel & Bungalow

Quiet setting with pool, located on the hillside. Rooms with air-conditioning. minibar, television. Good value for money. Five minutes from the beach. *126 rooms, Kata Beach, Patak Road, Tel. 076/33 06 03, Fax 33 08 95, e-mail peachill@phuket.ksc.co.th, Category 2*

Sansabai Bungalows

Simple bungalows with television, minibar, air-conditioning or fan. Quiet position near the centre, ten minutes walk from the beach. *32 rooms, Patong Beach, Soi Sansabai, Rat Uthit Road, Tel. 076/34 29 48, Fax 33 48 88, Category 2–3*

SPORTS & LEISURE

You can participate in virtually any kind of sport you choose here. Phuket is Thailand's tourist diving centre par excellence since the water quality in the Andaman Sea is generally better than in the Gulf of Siam. You can drive a go-cart (on the road between Patong and Phuket town), play mini-golf (at Patong and Kata), bowls (Phuket town), golf (several courses), shoot and go riding (Chalong). Several tour operators organize elephant trekking.

ENTERTAINMENT

The night-life for tourists is mainly concentrated at Patong

Beach where there are several ☆ discos *(Safari Pub, Shark Club, Titanic)*. Thais and Phuket's resident ex-pats favour the ◉ *Timber & Rock (Phuket town, Yaowaraj Road, open daily except Sundays from 10 pm)*. New on the scene and already proving a huge success is the *Fantasea* theme park *(Tel. 076/ 27 12 22, www.phuket-fantasea.com, entrance Bahts 1,000 or Bahts 1,500 including a sumptuous buffet dinner)*. Opened at Kamala Beach in 1999, as many as 3,000 visitors are entertained from 5.30 pm onwards each evening with a truly spectacular show including a herd of trained elephants. Pick-up service operated by its own fleet of minibuses.

INFORMATION

Tourism Authority of Thailand (TAT)

Also lots of brochures from private operators. *Open daily 8.30 am–4.30 pm, Phuket town, Phuket Road, Tel. 076/22 10 36, Fax 21 35 82*

Internet

www.phuket.com

SURROUNDING AREA

Khao Sok National Park (108/C 4–5)

☆ Not only is this the largest stretch of jungle remaining in the south, but the world's largest flower, genus *Rafflesia*, also blooms here. Boat trips run on the *Chieo Lan* Reservoir. You can even float down the *Sok River* in an inflated inner-tube with *Tubing*. Accommodation is mainly in bamboo hut resorts, for example in the tree houses of *Tree Tops Jungle Safaris (Tel. 01/723 14 87, 075/39 64 25, Fax 39 64 26, all-inclusive*

prices) or in the *Rainforest Resort (5 rooms, Tel. 01/64 43 62, 075 61 27 30, Fax 075/61 29 14, Category 3)*. Khao Sok National Park is situated on the mainland about halfway between Phuket and Surat Thani on the Gulf of Siam. You can take an organized tour or make your own arrangements.

Ko Phi Phi Don (108/C 6)

☆ Despite the fact that this tiny island brims over with tourists and day trippers, both it and its uninhabited twin *Ko Phi Phi Le* are of such dramatic beauty that it is still well worth taking a boat over from Phuket (or Krabi). In the colourful cobbled-together tourist village on the main (traffic-free) island, there are lots of dive centres and plenty of accommodation, for example the 50 bungalows at the *Phi Phi Pavilion (Tel. 075/61 12 95, Fax 62 06 33, Category 2)*. The *Phi Phi Island Village (80 rooms, Tel. 01/211 19 07, 076/21 50 14, Fax 076/21 49 18, Category 2)*, situated in a little bay with a palm-studded beach at *Loh Bagao*, offers perfect tropical island tranquility.

Phang Nga Bay (108/C 5)

☆ Here the limestone topography forms a weird landscape of cliffs, stacks and sugar-loaf islands rising as much as 300 metres out of the sea. *James Bond Island* got its name and became known to millions through *The Man With the Golden Gun* being filmed here. But the authorities would now like to bar tourists from the island for conservation reasons. Other sights include stalactitic caves and the pile-village on the island of *Ko Pannyi*. Whatever other excursions you plan, this extraordinary bay is one place you should make sure you see.

Jungle, palms and a luxury train

These routes are marked in green on the map on the inside front cover and in the Road Atlas beginning on page 98

① THROUGH THAILAND ON THE EASTERN & ORIENTAL EXPRESS

 This world-famous luxury train provides the most comfortable and elegant way of travelling from Singapore to Bangkok and on to Chiang Mai. The Express, the only one of its kind in South-East Asia, is a grand hotel on wheels, its thirteen sleeper carriages, two dining cars and saloon-, bar- and observation cars being beautifully appointed and solidly built in the style of the nineteen thirties. While being positively spoilt by the attentive service on the journey, you are able to delight in virtually the whole gamut of Thailand's varied landscapes as they pass by your window – rice paddies punctuated by coconut palms, rubber and pineapple plantations, bizarre karst formations and jungle-clad hillsides.

The Eastern & Oriental Express operates throughout the year, departing from Singapore most Wednesdays at 3.10 pm. After a stop in Butterworth (Malaysia) on the Thursday morning, the train finally arrives on Thai soil that afternoon. During Thursday night it makes its way along the narrow strip of land, in some places no more

than 10 km wide, between Myanmar (formerly Burma) and the Gulf of Thailand.

On arrival in *Kanchanaburi (page 49)* at 8.45 am on Friday morning, a visit to the famous bridge over the Kwai River, constructed by allied prisoners-of-war, is on the programme (depart again at 11.15 am). With lunch taken on the train, the Express draws into *Bangkok (page 32)* at 2.45 pm.

On certain Fridays between the end of September and April, the train continues on to Chiang Mai, leaving Bangkok at 7.30 pm. On the Saturday morning at 10.10 pm it pulls into the station at *Lampang*. Here, following breakfast, there is the option of visiting one of the surrounding villages or taking a drive in horse-drawn carriage, before departing once more at 11.30 am.

After Lampang the most impressive stretch of the railway begins, the train making its way downhill and through a 1,352 metre-long tunnel built in 1918 by German engineers. At 7.45 pm it finally reaches journey's end at *Chiang Mai (page 55)*.

② THE STILL TRADITIONAL NORTH – THE OTHER THAILAND

The round trip from Chiang Mai to Mae Hong Son, going clockwise, i.e. south to begin with, then back by the northern route, is one of the most spectacular and scenically most exciting in Thailand. It cuts through areas of almost virgin jungle, and snakes boldly over mountain passes. In this remote region, ethnic Thais make up only a small minority of the population. The hill tribes, whose women are often seen wearing their traditional costumes, comprise the dominant group. You should allow at least five days for the full journey, which you can undertake either by hire-car or bus – there are several buses a day. Road conditions are good in any season; nevertheless, you are advised to avoid travelling at night.

The H 108, the first 20 km or so being motorway, leaves *Chiang Mai (page 55)* and heads roughly south-westwards across a fertile plain, before following the course of the Ping River, out of sight to the left. Immediately before *Chom Thong*, the H 1009 branches off to *Doi Inthanon (page 58)*, the country's highest mountain. If you so fancy, you can hire one of the waiting *songtaeos* to take you to the summit, from where you enjoy marvellous distant views. Afterwards, turn right off the H 1009 below the summit onto the delightful H 1192, which ends after 22 km at *Mae Cham*. On the left the H 1088 leads back to the main H 108. If you don't want to make the detour to Doi Inthanon, simply continue on the H 108 through Chom Thong. Having reached the bridge where it crosses the Mae Nam Chaem,

the road sharply changes direction westwards. Here the kilometre marks restart at zero. After 11 km the road follows the Chaem River to a spot where its waters have broken through a rock barrier via a narrow gorge. From a wooden footbridge you can peer down 40 metres into the chasm below. The H 108 now turns onto a plateau, before, at the km 73 mark, winding its way down in a series of sharp bends to *Mae Sariang*, surrounded by orchards, where this first stage of the trip ends. In the town there are several simple hotels and guest houses, e.g. the *Riverside Guest House (Lhang Panich Road, Tel. 053/68 11 88, Category 3)*, offering simple accommodation in a splendid location overlooking the Yuam River.

At Mae Sariang the H 108 turns north across a landscape of hills and ravines. Beyond the km 234 mark, a steep, winding side road ascends to a transmitter station on the 2,000 m-high *Doi Nang Pu*. From here there are more superb views. After a further 22 km, hot sulpher springs can be seen on the left-hand side of the road. Continue over the top of the pass and down into the plain and the town of *Mae Hong Son (page 61)*, the end of the second stage. This remote provincial capital has developed into a busy recreational centre, with many trekking operators. The morning market, with the women dressed in their colourful traditional costumes, makes a wonderful sight. Hand-made wares produced by the hill tribes can be bought cheaply. The architecture of the temples here reveals clear Burmese influence.

Rooms are available in every price category.

Continuing north, now on the H 1095, before reaching the village of *Huai Pha* you can visit a grotto teeming with carp. You then drive over a pass to *Ban Mae Suya* (km 171), and shortly afterwards – having crossed a bridge over the Khong River – arrive at a forest lodge from where there are walks to seldom visited waterfalls and to *Tham Nam Lang*, one of the largest caves in the whole of Asia. The H 1095 now goes over wooded heights and through valleys with terraced rice paddies to *Soppong* (at km 140), the end of the third stage of the journey. Here the *Jungle House* (near the bus stop) and other guest houses offer simple accommodation and can help plan excursions. An 8 km minor road to the left ends at *Ban Tham*. The nearby *Tham Lot*, a cave with the Nam Lang flowing through it, warrants a visit just on account of the spectacle played out there each evening when literally thousands of swallows fly into the cave and just as many bats fly out.

From Soppong the H 1095 twists and turns in sharp bends over a pass, before descending 700 metres to the little town of *Pai*, the heart of the region and the penultimate stopping place. In the town there are pleasant places to spend the night. Some 9 km beyond Pai the H 1095 crosses the Pai River. After the bridge, a track branches off to the *Pong Son* hot springs (not suitable for bathing). Once through *Mae Sae*, the H 1095 winds spectacularly in a series of steep hairpin bends over a pass. At the km 42 mark an unsurfaced track leads to *Pong Duet*, hot

springs where water spouts metres into the air from the ground. At *Mae Tang* the H 1095 joins the H 107, here upgraded to a motorway, for the final stretch southwards to Chiang Mai.

③ THE HARSH NORTH-EAST

The arid north-east scarcely conforms to the usual image of a verdant and picturesque Thailand. Nevertheless, the more than 1,000 km drive from Bangkok to Nong Khai, on the frontier with Laos, is immensely rewarding on account of the many and varied things to be seen on the way: the Khao Yai National Park with its elephants, bears and leopards; the silk weavers' villages; and, no less interesting, the several very famous examples of classical Khmer architecture. The journey, which can be made either by car or bus, takes at least five days.

Leave Bangkok travelling north on the H 1 (motorway) and after 100 km branch eastwards onto the H 2, which begins here. Shortly before *Pak Chong* there is a turn-off for the *Khao Yai National Park*, some 40 km away. The park, lying to the south of the main road, covers an area of 2,168 sq km. With its evergreen rainforest and considerable numbers of animals, Khao Yai is one of the major conservation areas in South-East Asia. 200 elephants live here, as well as deer (including roe deer), wild boars, bears, tigers and leopards. The park administration arranges night safaris. However, there is no suitable accommodation in the park itself, the nearest place to stay being *Juldis Khao Yai Resort (54 Moo 4 Thanarat Road, Thambon Pak Chong Nakhon Ratchasima 30130, Tel. 044/29 72 97, Fax 29 72 91).*

Beyond Pak Chong the H 2 follows along the banks of a reservoir. Well before Nakhon Ratchasima (usually heard called Korat), there is a junction where the H 201 branches off to *Si Khiu*, continuing for a further 120 km through a largely monotonous stretch of country to the provincial capital of *Chaiyaphum*. The elephant show held here every January is only marginally less impressive than the much more famous one in Surin. In nearby *Ban Khai* the villagers earn their living taming and training elephants. The silk weavers of *Ban Khwao*, 13 km west of Chaiyaphum on the H 225, manufacture finely patterned fabrics of excellent quality. Chaiyaphum is the end of the second stage of the journey. A good place to spend the night is the *Hotel Lertnimitra (447/1 Nivestra Road, Tel. 044/81 15 22, Fax 82 23 35, Category 3)*, near the bus station. There are lots of buses to Korat.

Next, return along the H201 the way you came to rejoin the H 2 once again beyond Si Khui. Head east in the direction of Korat, but before long turn right onto the H 24 and on to *Pak Thong Chai*, another weaving village producing high grade silks with traditional patterns. Then a straight stretch of the H 24 goes to the small town of *Ban Ta Ko* and the turn-off to the Khmer temple of *Prasat Phanom Rung*. From there a road runs steeply downhill for another few kilometres to the imposing ruins of *Prasat Muang Tam*. Here the sculptures, especially those on the lintels of the doors to the towers and entrance chambers, display the greatest skill and artistry. From Prasat Muang Tam proceed via the village of *Chorake Mak* to *Prakhon*

Chai on the H 24. There you have the option of another detour, this time to *Surin (page 70)*, which is only really worthwhile at the time of the elephant round-up in November. Otherwise the route doubles back in the direction of Korat. At *Chok Chai*, the H 224 branches off to the potters' village of *Dan Kwian (page 68)*, where you can watch ceramic wares being manufactured. Next stop (to spend the night) is *Nakhon Ratchasima (page 67)*. Apart from good hotels the city has little of interest to offer tourists.

On the next stage of the journey the first port of call is *Phimai (page 68)*. Turning right off the H 2 some 44 km beyond Nakhon Ratchasima, follow the H 206 and then the H 2163 to reach the huge and immensely impressive *banyan tree* (known as *Sai Ngam*) and the exceptionally interesting *Prasat Hin Phimai* temple complex, a Khmer tower shrine dating from the 11th century.

At *Ban Phai*, on the H 2 some 46 km before *Khon Kaen*, the H 2057 branches left to *Chonnabot*, 16 km away, where the highly-valued heavy matmie silk is manufactured using traditional methods. This penultimate stage of the journey ends in *Khon Kaen (page 65)*, where the museum most definitely warrants a visit.

Leaving Khon Kaen, make your way via Udon Thani to *Ban Chiang (page 71)*, a must for anyone with an interest in prehistory. Here the remains of an advanced agrarian culture more than 6,000 years old have been uncovered. Journey's end is the town of *Nong Khai (page 69)* on the Mekong River, on the Thai–Laotian border. The return to Bangkok by express train takes eleven hours.

Practical information

*Useful addresses and essential information
for your visit to Thailand*

AMERICAN & BRITISH ENGLISH

Marco Polo travel guides are written in British English. In North America certain terms and usages deviate from British usage. Some of the more frequently encountered examples are (American given first):
baggage = luggage; cab = taxi; car rental = car hire; drugstore = chemist; fall = autumn; first floor = ground floor; freeway/highway = motorway; gas(oline) = petrol; railroad = railway; restroom = toilet/lavatory; streetcar = tram; subway = underground/tube; toll-free numbers = freephone numbers; trailer = caravan; trunk = boot (of a car); vacation = holiday; wait staff = waiter/waitress; zip code = post code.

AIRPORT CHARGES

A *passenger service charge* or *airport tax* of Bahts 30 is levied on inland flights. At Sukhothai and Ko Samui airports, built by the private Bangkok Airways, charges of Bahts 400 and 500 are payable on flights to inland and overseas destinations respectively.

BANKS & MONEY

The Thai *Baht* is divided into 100 *Satangs*. Notes to the value of Bahts 20 (green), 50 (blue), 100 (red), 500 (violet) and 1,000 (grey) are in general circulation, the brown 10-Baht notes having mostly been withdrawn. Coins of Bahts 1.5 and 10 are in normal use; the smaller Satangs 25 and 50 coins are usually seen only in supermarkets. Since exchange controls were lifted in July 1997 and the Baht became linked to the dollar, the currency has fluctuated wildly in value. There is no currency black market.

Traveller's cheques in sterling and US and Canadian dollars can be cashed at any bank. Normal bank opening hours are Monday to Friday 8.30 am to 3.30 pm, though on weekdays foreign exchange counters often stay open until 10 pm. In many shops a surcharge of a few per cent is imposed on credit card purchases. Though it is possible to draw cash on production of your passport, by far the most convenient method is via a cash machine or *ATM* (automatic teller machine). A *Visa* card is the most practical, being the most widely distributed as well as accepted by all major banks. *Mastercard* and *Eurocard* are also widely accepted but *American Express* cards can only be used to draw cash at branches of the *Bangkok Bank*.

The handling charge of a few per cent is paid by the credit card company or issuing bank. Best of all are cards which accept an interest-bearing credit balance, thus avoiding exceeding the borrowing limit.

Loss of a credit card should be reported immediately to the office of the relevant company in Bangkok: *American Express: Tel. 02/273 00 22, 273 00 44; Mastercard/Eurocard* and *Visa: 02/299 19 90–2, 02/273 74 48–9*

CAMPING

Designated camping sites are unknown in Thailand. However, tents are allowed in most National Parks.

CAR RENTAL

Even in remote areas roads are almost always surfaced. A rental car lends itself very well to exploring the provinces, but driving in Bangkok is recommended only for those with infinite patience and nerves of steel. There are many local car rental companies as well as international firms such as Avis and Hertz. A *Toyota Corolla* with air-conditioning costs approximately Bahts 1,800 a day, an open jeep between Bahts 800 and 1,000, with reductions for longer periods. Beware of small local rental companies touting their vehicles on the beaches, often without insurance cover.

An international driving licence is obligatory. Make certain you have comprehensive insurance covering both personal injury and damage to property. Since general insurance is not compulsory in Thailand, foreigners are often the losers irrespective of blame, being the only party from whom something can be recovered.

Anyone not used to driving on the left will find they quickly become adjusted to it – though not to the often suicidal standard of driving. As an alternative to

---

The Lady-men

In Thailand you will often come across women who were once men – or who still are under their feminine clothing. *Katoy* or *lady-men*, many of them exceptionally pretty, appear in lavishly-produced transvestite shows in Bangkok, Pattaya and Phuket. It can be quite hard to believe that the seductive creatures on stage are not actually women. And many a night-time reveller has been taken aback to discover that a generous bust measurement is no guarantee of one hundred per cent femininity. Not every katoy puts his admirer in the picture. Many transvestites are prostitutes, but many others pursue perfectly ordinary careers, a tribute to the tolerance of Thai society. True, the Thais find the lady-men amusing, but not in any spiteful or hurtful way. As for the katoy, they certainly don't keep themselves to themselves; on the contrary they will often deliberately seek the limelight and revel in the public gaze.

self-drive, cars can be rented at quite reasonable rates with a driver, e.g. for an additional cost of Bahts 600 for an eight-hour day.

CHILD PROTECTION

In the bar districts of Bangkok, Pattaya and Phuket children do the rounds of the bars at night selling chewing gum, cigarettes and flowers. In the view of the child protection agency *Childwatch Phuket (Tel. 076/20 25 59)*: "The more that is bought from them, the more certain it is that they will have to work until the early hours. No matter what big eyes the children make at you or how sorry you feel for them, it is actually better for them if you don't buy anything at all." And remember, it isn't dire need which turns five year-olds into night workers. This peddling of flowers and cigarettes is just as highly organized as is begging.

CUSTOMS

Currency to a value exceeding US$ 10,000 must be declared on entry. Items for personal use only can be taken in duty free, including, officially, a camera and a maximum of five rolls of film. However in this respect controls on entry are fairly relaxed and in our experience difficulties are unlikely to be encountered purely as a result of carrying more films. Weapons, drugs and pornography are strictly forbidden. The export of Buddha figures is also forbidden, and an export permit required for all antiques and animal products.

EMBASSIES

Canadian Embassy
15th Floor, Abdulrahim Place, 990 Rama, Bangrak, Bangkok 10501, Thailand, postal address P.O. Box 2090, Bangkok 10501, Tel. 02/636 05 40, Fax 636 05 55

British Embassy
1031 Wireless Road, Bangkok 10330, Tel. 02/253 01 91-9, Fax (consular) 255 60 51, www. britishemb.or.th

United States Embassy
95 Wireless Road, Bangkok 10330, Tel. 02/205 40 00, Fax 254 11 71

HEALTH

There are no statutory vaccination requirements. In jungle areas along the Myanmar and Cambodian frontiers there is a risk of malaria, but in our experience the risk is not great enough to warrant forgoing a trekking tour. Unprotected sex carries considerable risk of contracting venereal disease or even AIDS.

You should not drink tap water, though it is alright to clean your teeth with it. Even if risk of a stomach upset cannot entirely be excluded, it would be a shame to miss out on all the culinary delights in store wherever you go. Generally speaking food is prepared under hygienic conditions. You can find information on the Internet under *www.fit-for-travel.de*.

Medical care in the big cities is good. Bangkok and the main tourist centres have modern hospitals staffed by doctors trained in Europe and America, as do clinics and polyclinics. Though

The cloth of cloths

It can be worn as a head or a neck scarf, as a stole or a sash, or even as a short sarong; it protects as much against draughts as against the scorching sun; it can be tied in a bundle for carrying bits and pieces, or folded into a hammock for a baby; it makes a good handkerchief or a pad to cushion the head of anyone carrying a heavy weight. And just what is this all-purpose epitome of virtuosity? A *pa kao ma*; it measures about 130 mal 70 cm and is the most practical of Thai clothing. Particularly in country districts men as well as women still continue to set great store by this cloth of cloths. Usually red and white, or blue and red check, after many washes the colours do tend to fade; but by then the cloth has become wonderfully soft. Not only does a *pa kao ma* make a nice inexpensive souvenir, in contrast to many things you might purchase, it will prove extremely useful when travelling too.

hospitals provide dental care, independent dental practitioners are of a high standard and comparatively inexpensive – some tourists even combine a holiday with dental treatment. Medical bills must be settled by the patient (make sure you arrange appropriate health insurance before travelling). Almost all medicines are available from chemists without prescription and considerably cheaper than at home.

INFORMATION

Tourism Authority of Thailand (TAT) Offices

In Canada
55 University Ave 1208, Toronto, Ontario M5J 2H7, Tel.416/364-3363
2840 West 6th Ave, Vancouver, BC V6K 1X1, Tel. 604/733-4540

In the UK
49 Albemarle St, London W1X 3FE, Tel. 020 7499 7679

In the USA
303 E. Wacker Dr, Suite 400, Chicago, IL 60601, Tel. 312/819-3990
5 World Trade Center, Suite 3443, New York, NY 10048, Tel. 212/432-0433

In Thailand
In Thailand there are TAT offices in all the main provincial capitals. You can find their addresses in the relevant chapters of this guide.

NEWSPAPERS

The *Bangkok Post* and *The Nation*, both daily newspapers, provide full national and international coverage. The largest selection of English-language papers is found in the tourist centres.

PASSPORTS & VISAS

No visa is required for stays of up to 30 days. Passports must be valid for at least a further six months. For longer stays a *Tourist*

Visa is required, valid for 60 days, or where appropriate a *Non-Immigrant Visa*, valid for 90 days. For a cost of Bahts 500 it is possible to have a tourist visa extended by 30 days at *Immigration* in Bangkok and all the main provincial capitals and tourist centres. You will need to provide photocopies of the personal details page of your passport and your visa, and two passport photographs (photocopy shop next to *Immigration*). If you only want to prolong your stay by a few days, you can do so but will be charged Bahts 100 per day on leaving the country. Under no circumstance should you stay on for weeks beyond the expiry of your visa: to do so may incur a hefty fine or even imprisonment. Visas can be obtained from Thai embassies and consulates abroad.

In Canada

Royal Thai Embassy, 180 Island Park Drive, Ottawa, Ontario K1Y 0A2, Tel. 613/722–4444, Fax 613/722–6624; consular office open 9.30–11.30 am and 1.30–3 pm (closed most Thai and Canadian federal holidays)

Royal Thai Consulate-General, 1040 Burrad St, Vancouver, BC V6Z 2R9, Tel. 604/687–1143/8848, Fax 604/687–4434
e-mail info@thaicongenvancouver.org

In the UK

Royal Thai Embassy, 29–30 Queen's Gate, London, SW7 5JB, Tel. 020 7589 2944, Fax 020 7823 9695
e-mail thaiduto@btinternet.com

Royal Thai Consulate, Pacific House, 70 Wellington Street Glasgow G2 6SB, Tel. 0141 248 6677, Fax 0141 221 0255

In the USA

Royal Thai Embassy, 1024 Wisconsin Ave. N.W., Suite 401, Washington, D.C. 20007, Tel. 202/944–3600, Fax 202/944–3611
e-mail thai.wsn@thaiembdc.org

Royal Thai Consulate-General, 351 East 52nd St, New York, NY 10022 Tel. 212/754–1770/2536–8, Fax 212/754–1907

Royal Thai Consulate-General, 700 North Rush Street, Chicago, Il 60611, Tel. 312/236–2447, Fax 312/236–1906
e-mail thaichi@interaccess.com

Royal Thai Consulate-General, 801 North La Brea Ave., Los Angeles, CA 90038, Tel. 213/962–9574/9576, Fax 213/962–2128
e-mail thai-la@directnet.com

In addition to the addresses listed, Thailand maintains consular representation in other major cities in all three countries.

PHOTOGRAPHY

Before photographing people you should always politely ask their permission, or smile indicating your camera; that way you will rarely be refused. Colour film can be purchased everywhere and is generally somewhat cheaper than at home, as also is the cost of having films developed (1-hour service is standard, with prints returned in a small wallet). Slide films, on the other hand, cannot easily be obtained everywhere and are best brought with you from home.

POST

Air letters of up to 10 grams for

Rattletraps on three wheels: tuk-tuks

Europe and North America cost Bahts 17 and 19 respectively, post-cards a flat rate of Bahts 12. Most take between five and seven days to arrive. Tariffs for parcels are graduated according to weight and mode of transport (sea or air). To send a parcel weighing 5 kg by air costs about Bahts 1,200. Most post office sell the regulation packaging for parcels.

PUBLIC TRANSPORT

Rail, bus and air links are excellent and good value for money. A second class berth in a sleeping car from Bangkok to Chiang Mai for instance costs about Bahts 480, a flight from Bangkok to Phuket about Bahts 2,320. The air-conditioned VIP buses with couchettes (Bangkok to Phuket approximately Bahts 580) are comfortable. Local public transport consists mainly of (smaller or larger) *songtaeos* (literally: two benches), pick-up trucks or flat-bed lorries fitted

with a couple of benches. They have set fares.

TELEPHONE

The old coin-operated call boxes are being replaced increasingly by pay-card phones. Telephone cards to the value of Bahts 50, 100 and 200 can be purchased in post offices and from many shops. It is usually possible to make direct dialled calls abroad from rooms in better-class hotels, but many charge well above the official rate. At a post office or at the *Telecommunications Centre* a call to Europe costs Bahts 46 per minute. The dialling code for Canada and the United States is 1, for the United Kingdom 44. Those with mobile phones will find the connections good almost anywhere in Thailand. Information about tariffs can be obtained from the appropriate mobile phone company. To call Thailand from abroad dial 00 66 followed by the provincial dialling code, omitting the zero (e.g. for Phuket: 00 66 76).

TIME

Thailand is seven hours ahead of GMT and a further five hours ahead of Eastern Time (USA and Canada).

TIPPING

In very simple restaurants or at food stalls tipping is not customary. Many better-class restaurants levy a service charge of 10 per cent, in which case you should only tip if the service has been exceptionally good. Where no service charge is added, if the service is pleasant, a tip of 10 per cent is correct. Many hotels add a service charge of 10 per cent to the price of the room. Even then, porters and house boys appreciate a small note. It is not usual to tip taxi drivers, and definitely not if the price has been agreed in advance.

TOURIST POLICE

The Tourist Police have special responsibility for tourists. They can be contacted anywhere in the country by dialling:
Emergency number 1699

VALUE ADDED TAX

In many better-class shops, restaurants and hotels, VAT is charged at 10 per cent. In others VAT is included. Where VAT is charged, this will normally be stated, e.g. on menus and hotel price lists.

VOLTAGE

The voltage in Thailand is 220 volts. Plugs are the flat pin type. Adapters can be bought in electrical shops.

WEIGHTS & MEASURES

1 cm	0.39 inch
1 m	1.09 yd (3.28 ft)
1 km	0.62 miles
1 sq m	1.20 sq yds
1 ha	2.47 acres
1 sq km	0.39 sq miles
1 g	0.035 ounces
1 kg	2.21 pounds
1 British ton	1016 kg
1 US ton	907 kg

1 litre is equivalent to 0.22 Imperial gallons and 0.26 US gallons

WHEN TO GO

In the *cool* season from November to February temperatures seldom reach as high as 20°C at night or much over 30°C by day. From then on, until about the middle of May, it becomes very hot, with day-time temperatures as high as 35°C and night-time ones not much lower than 25°C. In the north and north-east the night-time temperatures during the cool season may drop as low as 15°C or even 10°C, while in the hot period day-time temperatures can reach 40°C.

During the rainy period from May to October the temperatures drop back somewhat; humidity, on the other hand is high and energy-sapping. The sea is at its calmest from December/January to March/April. During the monsoon period it often does rain for a few hours during the day; on the other hand it may not rain at all for days, though the sky may well be leaden. The wettest time of the year is from about mid August to mid October.

On Ko Samui there are two rainy seasons, the island being affected from November/December to mid February by secondary depressions associated with the north-east monsoon, an effect felt more especially on the east coast of Malaysia. However, the normal rainy season from August to October is less pronounced here than elsewhere in the country, so northern hemisphere spring and summer are actually the best time to visit the island.

If planning a beach holiday during the monsoon period, bear in mind that swimming in the choppy seas can be dangerous. This is particularly true of Phuket; tragically every year some tourists and Thais ignore the warnings and pay with their lives. It cannot be emphasized too strongly that any warnings should be observed.

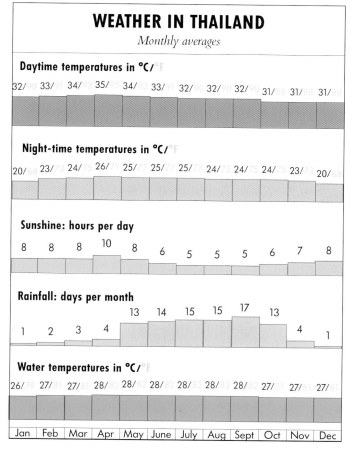

WEATHER IN THAILAND
Monthly averages

Daytime temperatures in °C/°F

Jan	Feb	Mar	Apr	May	June	July	Aug	Sept	Oct	Nov	Dec
32/90	33/91	34/93	35/95	34/93	33/91	32/90	32/90	32/90	31/88	31/88	31/88

Night-time temperatures in °C/°F

Jan	Feb	Mar	Apr	May	June	July	Aug	Sept	Oct	Nov	Dec
20/68	23/73	24/75	26/79	25/77	25/77	25/77	24/75	24/75	24/75	23/73	20/68

Sunshine: hours per day

Jan	Feb	Mar	Apr	May	June	July	Aug	Sept	Oct	Nov	Dec
8	8	8	10	8	6	5	5	5	6	7	8

Rainfall: days per month

Jan	Feb	Mar	Apr	May	June	July	Aug	Sept	Oct	Nov	Dec
1	2	3	4	13	14	15	15	17	13	4	1

Water temperatures in °C/°F

Jan	Feb	Mar	Apr	May	June	July	Aug	Sept	Oct	Nov	Dec
26/79	27/81	27/81	28/82	28/82	28/82	28/82	28/82	28/82	27/81	27/81	27/81

Do's and don'ts

What you should and should not do – tips for avoiding any unpleasantness

Encouraging envy or being provocative

Thailand is not in general a dangerous country to travel in. Even late at night you can feel safe in Bangkok. But a few precautions are appropriate here as anywhere in the world. Don't for example flaunt a bulging wallet. Women should not go topless on lonely beaches (and remember nudism is prohibited altogether). Avoid walking unescorted on beaches at night. Always keep an eye on luggage, especially in bus stations and other busy places.

Dealing in drugs

In the worst instance dealing in drugs is punishable by death. Though no Western foreigner has yet been executed, long-term detention in a Thai gaol is scarcely more inviting than a death sentence. So be warned: being found in possession of even the smallest quantities of soft drugs like *ganja* (marihuana) can lead to imprisonment!

Hiring vehicles on the street

In many holiday resorts cars and motor cycles are available for instant hire, without the "inconvenience" of a hire agreement – you only have to deposit your passport. As often as not such vehicles turn out to be damaged or defective and the innocent tourist is then forced to pay. It has even been known for cars or motor cycle to be "stolen" using a duplicate key, the tourist again being required to pay compensation for its loss. Always insist on a proper hire agreement (in English) and study the small print very carefully – what may look like favourable terms can in the end cost you dear.

Avoiding touts

Wherever there are tourists there will always be touts hanging around, with "irresistible" offers of every possible kind – bargain gemstones, free sightseeing tours, prostitutes … you name it, they can supply it! Don't be drawn into anything! The Thais generally are reserved when it comes to foreigners and do not simply speak to them on the street. So if someone does approach you, you can be quite sure it will be you who ends up with the worst of the deal.

Getting into an argument

In rare cases it can happen that even the otherwise very self-disciplined Thais can become hostile, perhaps as a result of having a drop too much to drink. Invitations to join in a drinking spree with people you don't know should be declined in a friendly way; or, if a drink is forced on you, leave after a polite sip. If nevertheless someone becomes aggressive, at all costs keep calm yourself. And whatever you do, avoid causing an already angry individual to lose face.

Road Atlas of Thailand

*Please refer to back cover for an overview
of this Road Atlas*

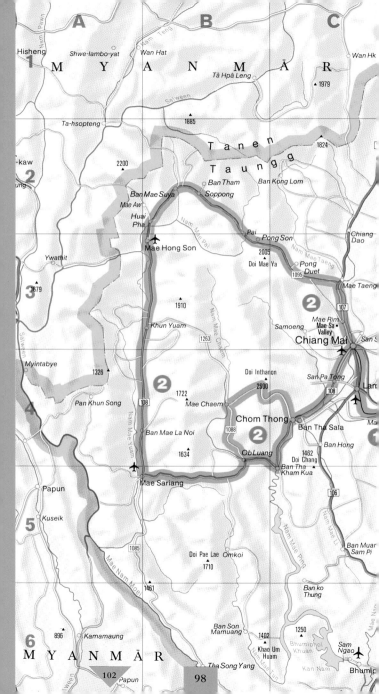

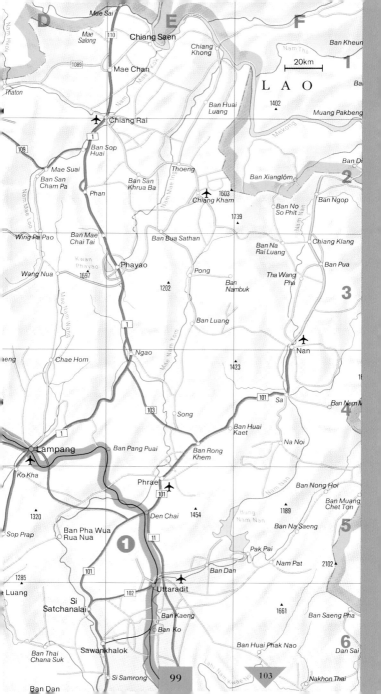

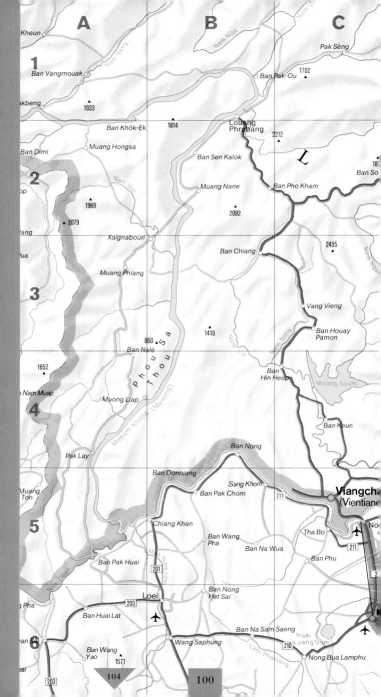

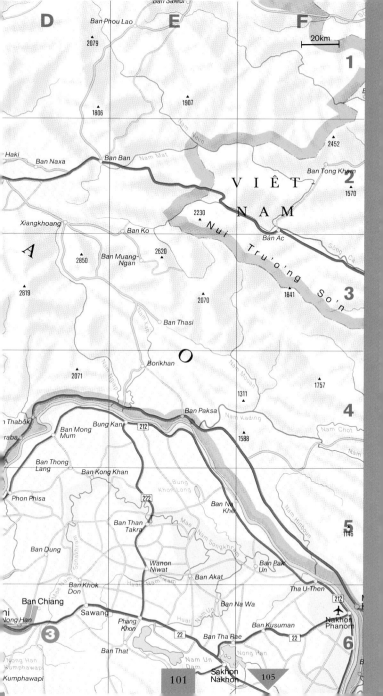

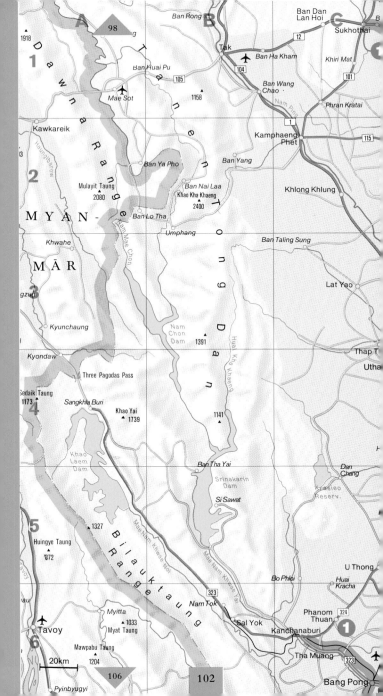

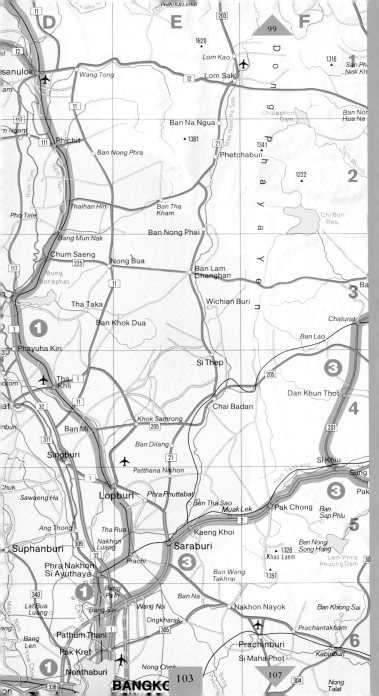

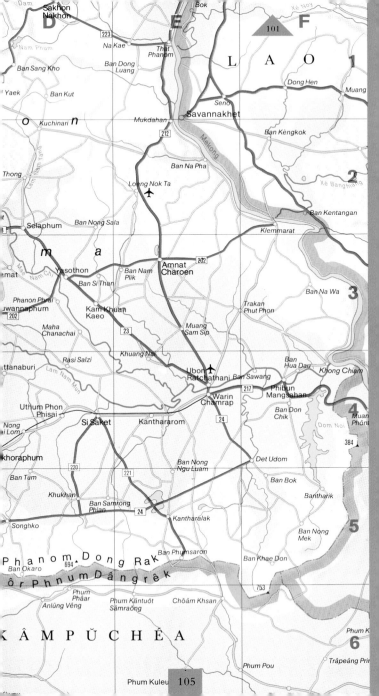

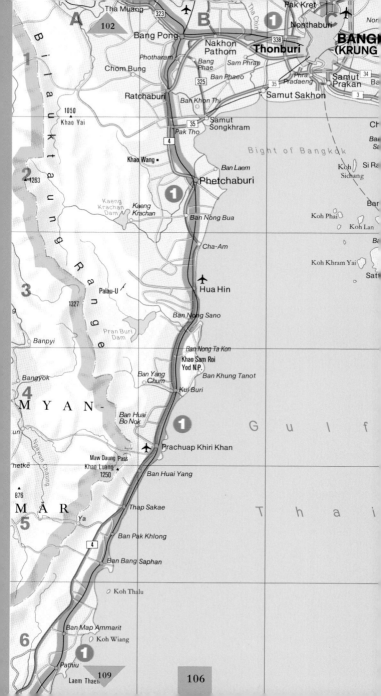

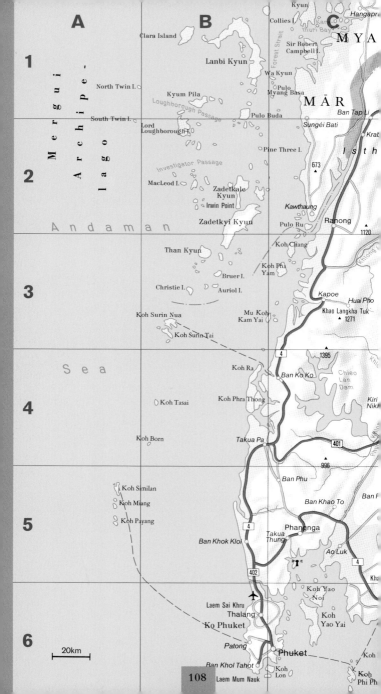

A

B

C

Clara Island

Kyun
Collies I.
Hangapr
Sir Robert
Campbell I.
M Y A

1

Lanbi Kyun
Wa Kyun
Pulo
Myang Basa

North Twin I.
Kyum Pila
M Ā R
Ban Tap Li

Mergui Archipe-lago

Loughborough Passage
Pulo Buda

South Twin I.
Lord
Loughborough I.
Sungéi Bati
Krat

Pine Three I.
673
I s t h

2

Investigator Passage

MacLeod I.
Zadetkale
Kyun
Kawthaung

Irwin Point
Pulo Ru
Ranong

Zadetkyi Kyun
1120

A n d a m a n

Than Kyun
Koh Chang

Koh Pha
Yam

Bruer I.

3

Christie I.
Auriol I.

Kapoe
Huai Pho

Koh Surin Nua
Mu Koh
Kam Yai
Khao Langkha Tuk
1271

Koh Surin Tai
1395

S e a
Koh Ra
Ban Ko Ko
Chieo
Lan
Dam

4

Koh Tasai
Koh Phra Thong
Kiri
Niki

Koh Born
Takua Pa
401

996

Ban Phu

Koh Similan
Ban Khao To
Ban F

5

Koh Miang
Phangnga

Koh Payang
Takua
Thung
Ao Luk

Ban Khok Kloi
4

402
Koh Yao
Noi

Laem Sai Khru
Koh
Yao Yai

Thalang
Ko Phuket

Patong
Koh

6

20km
Phuket

Ban Khol Tahot
Koh
Lon
Koh
Phi Ph

Laem Mum Nauk

108

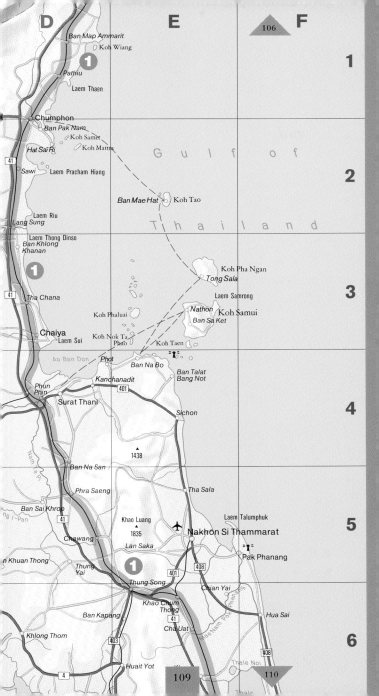

1

Ban Map Ammarit
Koh Wiang
Pathiu
Laem Thaen

Chumphon
Ban Pak Nam
Koh Samet
Hat Sai Ri
Koh Mattra
Sawi   Laem Pracham Hiang

2

G u l f   o f

Ban Mae Hat   Koh Tao

T h a i l a n d

Laem Riu
Lang Sung
Laem Thong Dinso
Ban Khlong
Khanan

Koh Pha Ngan
Tong Sala

Tha Chana
Laem Samrong

Nathon   Koh Samui
Koh Phaluai
Ban Sa Ket

3

Chaiya
Laem Sui
Koh Nok Ta
Koh Taen
Phao

Ao Ban Don
Phot
Ban Na Bo
Ban Talat
Bang Not

Phun
Phin
Kanchanadit

Surat Thani
Sichon

4

▲
1438

Ban Na San

Phra Saeng
Tha Sala

Ban Sai Khrop
ng i-Pan

Laem Talumphuk

Khao Luang
▲
1835
Nakhon Si Thammarat

Chawang
Lan Saka

5

n Khuan Thong
Pak Phanang

Thung
Yai
Thung Song

Khao Chum
Thong
Chian Yai

Ban Kapang
Hua Sai

Khlong Thom
Cha Uat

6

Huait Yot

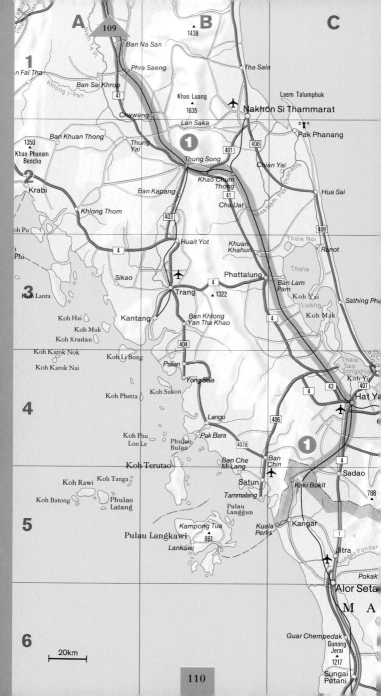

109

▲ 1438

Ban Na San

Phra Saeng

Tha Sala

Khong I-Pan

Ban Fai Tha

Ban Sai Khrop

41

Khao Luang
1835

Laem Talumphuk

Nakhon Si Thammarat

Chawang

Lan Saka

Pak Phanang

Ban Khuan Thong

1350
Khao Phanom
Bencha

Thung
Yai

Thung Song

401

408

Krabi

Khao Chum
Thong

Chian Yai

Ban Kapang

41

Hua Sai

Khlong Thom

Cha Uat

403

Huait Yot

Khuan
Khahun

Thale Noi

408

4

Ranot

Koh Pu

Sikao

1322

Phattalung

Thale

Koh Lanta

Trang

Ban Lam
Pam

Koh Yai
Luang

Sathing Ph

Koh Hai

Kantang

Ban Khlong
Yan Tha Khao

Koh Mak

Koh Muk

Koh Kradan

4

Koh Karok Nok

Koh Li Bong

404

Koh Karok Nai

Palian

Thale
Sap
Songkhla

Yong Sala

Koh Yo

Koh Phetra

Koh Sukon

4

43

407

Hat Y

Langu

406

Koh Phu
Lon Le

Phulao
Bulan

Pak Bara

4

Koh Terutao

4078

Ban Che
Mi Lang

Ban
Chin

Koh Rawi

Koh Tanga

Satun

Kaki Bukit

Sadao

Koh Batong

Phulao
Latang

Tammalang

788

Pulau
Langgun

Kuala
Perlis

Kangar

Pulau Langkawi

Kampong Tua

881

Lankawi

1

Jitra

Sungei Pandar

Pokak

Alor Seta

M A

Guar Chempedak

Gunong
Jerai
1217

Sungai
Petani

20km

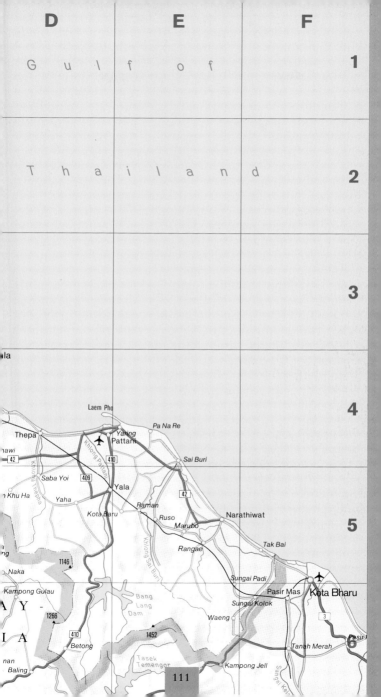

D   E   F

1

Gulf of

Thailand

2

3

la

4

Laem Pho

Thepa   Pa Na Re

Yaring
Pattani

nawi

42   Khlong Pattani   410   Sai Buri

Saba Yoi   409

Khlong Thepha

n Khu Ha   Yala

Yaha

Kota Baru   Raman

Ruso

Marubo   Narathiwat

Khlong Sai Buri

Rangae

ng

Naka   1146

Kampong Gulau

A Y -

1266

I A

nan

Baling   410   Betong

42

Tak Bai

Sungai Padi

Pasir Mas   Kota Bharu

Sungai Kolok

Waeng

3

1452

Tanah Merah

Tasek
Temengor   Kampong Jell

Sungai Kel

5

Bang
Lang
Dam

sir

6

111

ROAD ATLAS LEGEND

Autobahn mit Anschlußstelle	══════	Motorway with junction
Autobahn in Bau	═ ═ ═ ═	Motorway under construction
Wichtige Hauptstraße	▬▬▬▬	Important main road
Hauptstraße	────	Main road
Sonstige Straße	────	Other road
Eisenbahn	────	Railway
Straßennummer	─[15]─	Road number
Schiffahrtslinie	─ ─ ─ ─	Shipping route

Bergspitze mit Höhenangabe in Metern	4807 ▲	Mountain summit with height in metres
Leuchtturm	⌁	Lighthouse
Ruinenstätte	⋰	Ruins
Verkehrsflughafen	✈	Airport
Paß	) (	Pass
Staatsgrenze	▬▬▬	National boundary

Einwohnerzahl:	Population:
unter 100.000	less than 100.000
100.000 - 250.000	100.000 - 250.000
über 250.000	more than 250.000

20 km

INDEX

This index lists all the places, islands, sights and excursion destinations mentioned in this guide. Numbers in bold indicate a main entry, italics a photograph.

What do you get for your money?

With the Baht no longer linked to the US dollar, recent movements in exchange rates have been to the advantage of harder currencies. So despite prices being generally on the increase, Thailand has actually become cheaper for tourists. Rates at airport bureaux de change tend to be somewhat less favourable, so on arrival change only enough for immediate needs. Wait until you reach your holiday resort before changing larger sums.

Hotel prices vary enormously in Thailand. Phuket is by far the most expensive, but even here it should be possible to find a room in a hotel with a pool for about Bahts 2,000, or a room with air conditioning for

about Bahts 1,000. Bangkok is a bit cheaper, while in the north and north-east of the country and in Pattaya you should expect a fair degree of luxury for Bahts 1,000 to 2,000. And wherever you are, accommodation without air conditioning will be available for Bahts 400, often substantially less.

A bowl of noodle soup from a snack bar costs about Bahts 30, a rice dish with meat and vegetables in a no-frills restaurant about Bahts 50. A two-course meal including a pudding seldom exceeds Bahts 250. For a small bottle of beer brewed in Thailand you can expect to pay Bahts 30 to 40 in a supermarket and upwards of Bahts 50 in a restaurant. A litre of super grade petrol costs just Bahts 11.

US $	Baht	£	Baht	Can $	Baht
1	39	1	59	1	27
2	78	2	118	2	54
3	117	3	177	3	81
4	156	4	236	4	108
5	195	5	295	5	135
10	390	10	590	10	270
15	585	15	885	15	405
20	780	20	1,180	20	540
25	975	25	1,475	25	675
30	1,170	30	1,770	30	810
40	1,560	40	2,360	40	1,080
50	1,950	50	2,950	50	1,350
60	2,340	60	3,540	60	1,620
70	2,730	70	4,130	70	1,890
80	3,120	80	4,720	80	2,160
90	3,510	90	5,310	90	2,430
100	3,900	100	5,900	100	2,700
200	7,800	200	11,800	200	5,400
300	11,700	300	17,700	300	8,100
400	15,600	400	23,600	400	10,800
500	19,500	500	29,500	500	13,500
750	29,250	750	44,250	750	20,250
1,000	39,000	1,000	59,000	1,000	27,000

These exchange rates are for guidance only and are correct at the present time June 2000. You are advised to check with a bank or tourist office before travelling.